DULEEP SINGH'S STATUE

DULEEP SINGH'S STATUE

East Anglia's Lost Maharajah

Fraser Harrison

Signal Books
Oxford

First published in 2018 by
Signal Books Limited
36 Minster Road
Oxford OX4 1LY
www.signalbooks.co.uk

A catalogue record for this book is available from the British Library

ISBN 978-1-909930-66-7 Paper

Cover Design: Tora Kelly
Typesetting: Tora Kelly
Front Cover Image: Fraser Harrison
Back Cover Image: 'Casualty of War', A Portrait of Maharajah Duleep Singh copyright The Singh Twins www.singhtwins.co.uk
Title page, chapter headings, page-break artwork: copyright The Singh Twins www.singhtwins.co.uk
Printed in India by Imprint Digital Ltd

For Tilly and Jack,
with much love

CONTENTS

PART ONE

ONE
A SUNNY DAY IN MAY

It is a sunny day in May, and I am in Thetford in the county of Norfolk.

I am walking through the town's shopping centre, a single, unlovely, pedestrianised street where, however, you can buy Portuguese custard tarts, Lithuanian beer and smoked meats from Poland. The fragrance of barbecued sausages drifts from J. Jones, a butcher's named in honour of the hero of *Dad's Army*. At the end of the street I turn left and pause for a moment to lean on the rail of the town's main bridge, a single cast-iron span built in 1829. On the far side I can see the grammar school where Thomas Paine, born nearby, used to toil over his books in its cold, damp schoolroom. Below me are the sedate waters of the Little Ouse. Downstream, the river is framed by drooping willows in a picturesque vignette, its canalised course receding and narrowing like a lesson in perspective as it flows westwards to join the Great Ouse. I turn back to walk along the concrete terrace that gives shoppers a place to sit and contemplate Thetford's riverfront. Finally, I cross the river by another of the town's many bridges. This is a three-legged footbridge that offers people the choice of turning towards the new cinema-hotel complex and its car park, or turning the other way to make landfall on Butten Island, a sliver of ground created by the Little Ouse and its tributary, the Thet, which run parallel for a few hundred yards.

In effect Butten Island is a miniature park, and it is the prettiest part of Thetford. I have my camera at the ready. Swans glide on the smooth water, while a gaggle of Canadian geese, identifiable by their perfectly laundered white chin straps, occupies the bank. The adults hover at the edge of the group, their long necks tensely upright as they keep watch over their goslings, a dozen portly adolescents cropping the grass with fuzzy down still clinging to their backs. But I am not here to photograph them. I am looking for a good place to take a picture of the statue that stands in the middle of the island, and is now framed by trees in their freshest leaf. The subject of this life-size bronze statue is a man on a horse; he carries a sword, wears a turban and sports a fine beard with curling moustaches. The statue itself stands on a plinth of polished black granite that is as tall as the horse and its exotic rider, who must surely have ridden a great distance before arriving in Thetford.

Most people walk past the statue without giving it a glance; some look up for a moment, as if to make contact with an acquaintance whom they see every day but never speak to. A few people, strangers to the town or newcomers, leave the path to take a casual look at the statue and the inscription on its plinth before wandering away. On this occasion a group of adults and children, perhaps a couple of families, has gathered round the statue. While the children play and shout, the adults stare intently at the figure on his horse, and read every word of the inscription. They go round the plinth to read the inscription on the other side, which is written in a different script. Several of the men wear turbans and have allowed their beards to grow long; the women wear saris. One of the older men, whose grey whiskers are unusually abundant, calls the children to gather round the statue, and out of deference to their parents' serious mood they look up at the figure respectfully for a moment, before running off again.

The words on the plinth, which are engraved in gold letters on the surface of the black marble, are as follows:

"BRINGING HISTORY AND CULTURES TOGETHER"

THIS PLAQUE COMMEMORATES THE OFFICAL UNVEILING OF THIS MONUMENT BY H.R.H. THE PRINCE OF WALES, K.G.K.T. ON 29TH JULY 1999.

IN 1843 MAHARAJAH DULEEP SINGH SUCCEEDED HIS FATHER TO THE THRONE

OF THE SOVEREIGN SIKH KINGDOM OF PUNJAB. HE WAS DESTINED TO BE ITS LAST RULER.

IN 1849 FOLLOWING THE CLOSELY FOUGHT ANGLO-SIKH WARS THE BRITISH ANNEXED THE PUNJAB. DULEEP SINGH WAS COMPELLED TO RESIGN HIS SOVEREIGN RIGHTS AND EXILED. IT WAS AT THIS TIME THAT THE KOH-I-NOOR DIAMOND, LATER TO BE INCORPORATED INTO THE CROWN JEWELS, PASSED TO THE BRITISH AUTHORITIES.

DULEEP SINGH EVENTUALLY CAME TO BRITAIN AND SETTLED AT THE ELVEDEN ESTATE IN SUFFOLK. HE WAS A CLOSE FAVOURITE OF QUEEN VICTORIA AND BECAME A PROMINENT LOCAL FIGURE IN EAST ANGLIA.

LATER IN LIFE HE ANNOUNCED HIS INTENTION TO RETURN TO HIS BELOVED PUNJAB BUT WAS NOT ALLOWED TO DO SO. HE DIED IN PARIS ON OCTOBER 22ND 1893 HAVING RE-EMBRACED THE SIKH FAITH AND WHILST STILL ENGAGED IN A STRUGGLE TO REGAIN HIS THRONE.

TO THIS DAY THE SIKH NATION ASPIRES TO REGAIN ITS SOVEREIGNTY.

The last line is not easy to read because the statue appears to have sunk into the ground, nearly burying the letters beneath the grass.

So, the bronze horseman is Duleep Singh, last Maharajah of the Sikh kingdom of the Punjab, and we may reasonably guess that the visitors are themselves Sikhs. Yes, they have driven from Southall in London, and next they are planning to see Duleep Singh's grave in Elveden. Is it far away? I reassure them that the village is only a few miles distant, and that the graves are easy to locate in the churchyard. They take a few last pictures, gather up their boisterous children, and depart on the next leg of their pilgrimage.

Two

THE DISPOSSESSION OF DULEEP SINGH

I am left alone with the statue. Over the last two years I have been here many times, and my book is the fruit of those visits. The bronze Maharajah on his horse is a puzzle, and the inscription on its plinth, though purporting to explain its subject, only adds to the puzzle. For example, why does a large, costly statue of 'the last ruler of the Sikh kingdom of the Punjab' stand in Thetford, a town of more than 24,000 people among whom only twenty-four describe themselves as Sikhs?[i] And what impels so many Sikhs, like the family I have just met, to make the journey from the Midlands, London and elsewhere to see the statue? Why is it so important to them?

My subject is the statue of Duleep Singh, not the man himself, but to understand the statue it is necessary to know a little more about the Maharajah's extraordinary story than the handful of carefully selected facts inscribed on the plinth. Indeed, my book might be seen as an attempt to construe that gilded text.

Anyone who wants to read about the Maharajah and his family in detail is fortunate in having a choice of several excellent biographies. (See Appendix I.)

One thing these books have in common is that, with a single exception, their authors are British. Other biographies have been written by Indian authors and published in India, but they are of course less accessible to British readers. Though not a Sikh, I too am British, and my little book is an all-British affair. The statue in Thetford was made by a British sculptor, and her subject was a Sikh who lived most of his life in Britain. It stands in an English town, and it was paid for by the Sikh community in Britain.

However, I hope the book cannot be accused of bias towards British interests; on the contrary, if the piece has villains they are British. No one emerges well from the Duleep Singh story, with the possible exception of the Maharajah's British guardian and his wife, though they too were the instruments of British policy, and in that sense far from innocent. Duleep Singh was sometimes eager to cast himself in the role of victim, and there is no question that he was badly treated both in childhood and later, but as an adult he made crucial decisions for which he alone was responsible, and which in many cases were foolish or selfish.

It is a sorry tale, but thanks to the biographies I have mentioned, I feel at liberty to confine myself to a short account of Duleep Singh's life, and this comprises Part One. My sketch does draw attention to certain themes in his life, notably the punitive nature of his surrender, that help to explain the design of the statue and its significance. Part Two tells the story of the statue: how it was commissioned, how it came to be sited on Butten Island in Thetford, and how it has been received.

A curiosity of the plaque's inscription, one of several, is that it does not give the date of Duleep Singh's birth, which was 6 September 1838.

He was born in Lahore, the youngest son of Ranjit Singh (1780-1839), the so-called 'Lion of the Punjab', and it was his father who created the 'sovereign Sikh kingdom of Punjab' referred to in the second paragraph of the statue's inscription.

But who are, and who were the Sikhs?

Today, we in Britain tend to think of the Sikhs, the men at least, as Indians with turbans. In fact, the wearing of turbans is by no means exclusive to Sikhs, nor is it a reliable sign of identification. For the Sikhs, however, the turban carries a particular religious meaning, and for a devout Sikh wearing a turban is obligatory.

British Sikhs have made themselves well-known in this country as the people who have fought over the years for the right to wear their turbans at work and in schools, and to wear them instead of crash helmets and hard hats. The key case was *Mandla v Dowell-Lee*, in which a schoolboy in Edgbaston complained of racial discrimination when he was refused entry to his school for wearing a turban. The case went to the House of Lords in 1983, and the schoolboy's complaint was upheld. The verdict confirmed that Sikhs belonged to a separate 'ethno-religious group', a classification they shared with Jews, which had the advantage of bringing them under the protection of the Race Relations Act. They qualified because the court held that they fulfilled two essential conditions. As a group, the Sikhs had 'a long shared history, of which the group is conscious as distinguishing it from other groups, and the memory of which it keeps alive.' Secondly, the group had 'a cultural tradition of its own, including family and social customs and manners, often but not necessarily associated with religious observance.'[ii]

In his judgement Lord Templeman made some interesting comments on the question of the Sikhs' identity: 'They are more than a religious sect, they are almost a race and almost a nation... As a nation the Sikhs defeated the Moghuls, and established a kingdom in the Punjab which they lost as a result of the first and second Sikh wars. They fail to qualify as a separate nation or as a separate nationality because their kingdom never achieved a sufficient degree of recognition or permanence.'[iii] He had read his history and put his finger on the issue that haunts the Sikhs; his words may be heard to echo poignantly throughout this book

A belief in Sikhism is at the core of Sikh identity. Sikhism owes its original inspiration to Baba Nanak (1469-1539), who was born into a relatively affluent Punjabi family and received a good education. Nanak effectively turned his back on both Hinduism and Islam, and preached the idea of a single universal God, a formless, invisible, all-powerful divinity, who was the sole creator of everything that existed. At the same time he introduced a belief system that demanded of its followers that they both worshipped God and served their community, the *panth*, which was to be based on the principles of brotherhood, tolerance and equality. 'All humans are one,' he said, 'but superfluous misunderstandings are many.'[iv]

Under Nanak's influence, social justice was seen as a means to promoting prosperity and well-being; ethical behaviour was valued over ceremony, and selfless public service was regarded as a great virtue. Nanak ensured that the principle of equality was extended to women, and families were encouraged to educate their girls. In the same spirit, Nanak introduced the practice of *langar* or communal eating, a simple but radical way of defying the caste system: everyone ate together, seated on the floor, and all comers, regardless of caste or background, were served. The langar has continued to be a distinctive feature of all *gurdwaras*, or Sikh temples, and it is said that on religious holidays and weekends the kitchens of the Golden Temple in Amritsar feed 100,000 people a day.

The principles of Sikhism continued to be developed by the nine Gurus who succeeded Nanak, and they were gathered into a sacred scripture known as the Guru Granth Sahib. During the seventeenth century the Sikhs endured persecution from many sides. When the Mughal emperor, Aurangzeb (1618-1707), introduced a policy of compulsory conversion to Islam, which was cruelly enforced, the Sikhs adopted a warrior ethic, which was embedded in their creed. They became a military and a militant community. As the tenth Guru famously decreed, 'when all efforts to restore peace prove useless and no words avail, lawful is the flash of steel, it is right to draw the sword.'[v]

It was this same Guru, Gobind Singh, who formalised the religion in 1699 with a mass baptism, giving its community of believers, the khalsa, an institutional strength and coherence. The occasion saw the 'birth of a new and martial race,' according to the historian Patwant Singh, who estimates that 50,000 Sikhs, at least, were baptised at this time.[vi] The water used in the baptism ritual was sweetened with sugar and then stirred with a sword, a meld of sweetness and steel signifying that the khalsa was both a religious and a warrior community. The men were given a new surname, Singh, meaning lion, and in due course female members of the *khalsa* took the name Kaur, meaning princess. This commonality of names may be the bane of indexers, but it was another means of equalising the members of the panth, because it eliminated the possibility of identifying people's caste from their name; all were lions and princesses.

Gobind Singh also introduced the so-called five Ks, which have become the distinguishing features of Sikh men ever since. They were instructed to leave their hair uncut (*kesh*), to carry a wooden comb (*kangha*), to wear an iron or steel bracelet on their wrist (*kara*), to carry a short sword or dagger (*kirpan*) and to wear short breeches called *kachh* or *kacchera*. These innovations carried both sacred and war-like significance. The comb, while preventing long hair from becoming unkempt, was also a symbol of cleanliness and disciplined holiness. In the same way, the breeches were hygienic, but also served as a reminder of the need for sexual continence and moral restraint. The steel band both protected the arm that wielded the sword and symbolised the circular, wheel-shaped *dharma*, an ancient concept with many meanings in Indian religions, but adopted by the Sikhs as a reminder of the path of righteousness. It was sometimes called a 'handcuff to God.' The sword represented the call to uphold justice and protect the weak, and it was also was a symbol of Sikhs' readiness to fight for their religion and identity. To quote a historian of the time, 'The orchard of the Sikh faith needed the thorny hedge of armed men for its protection.'[vii]

Always a small minority, the Sikhs maintained a cohesive community, tied together by their beliefs and customs, as well as familial ties. From the outset they were determined to preserve their unique culture. Their resolution was put to the test many times during the eighteenth century when they suffered persecution and aggression on three sides, from the Mughal emperor, the

Afghan king, and the Shah of Persia. It has been reckoned that during the first seventy years of the eighteenth century a total of around 200,000 Sikhs were killed. Among the persistent bloodshed and torture, two massacres stand out. The first took place in 1746 when Mughal troops killed 7,000 Sikhs in a series of running battles and captured an additional 3,000, who were marched back to Lahore, paraded in the streets and publicly beheaded. The second, which occurred in April 1762, has been known ever since as the *Wada ghalughara* – the great massacre. The Afghan emperor, Ahmed Shah Abdali, descended on a great gathering of Sikh families, killing 25,000 to 30,000, and then dragged hundreds of Sikh prisoners in chains to Lahore. Next he attacked Amritsar, where several thousand Sikhs had gathered for a religious celebration, and ordered the Golden Temple to be blown up with gunpowder. The pool was filled with rubble, human bodies and, as a deliberate insult, the carcasses of cows. Finally, Abdali ordered that a pyramid of Sikh heads should be erected on the ruins of the temple.

Throughout these terrible years the Sikhs learnt how to be both farmers and warriors, always ready to drop their tools and take up the sword in defence of the panth. The men were formed into *misls*, military groups drawn from a particular village and owing allegiance to a local leader, who could be likened to a medieval English baron. The misl warrior was mounted on his own horse and was armed with his own sword and matchlock rifle. Infantry and artillery did not enjoy the same standing as these mounted soldiers. Inspired with religious and patriotic zeal, Sikh cavalrymen were feared for their agility and skill. 'They looked down on the comforts of the tents, carrying their and their animals' rations of grains in a knapsack, and with two blankets under the saddle as their bedding, they marched off with lightning rapidity in and out of battle.'[viii]

Showing extraordinary resilience, the Sikhs regained control of Amritsar and restored the temple after its desecration in 1762. Within three years they had annexed Lahore, the most powerful city in the Punjab, and were able to declare their control over the entire region in defiance of Mughal rule. Their military strength was reinforced by economic prosperity. With its five rivers, the Punjab was fertile, and during periods of peaceful stability Sikh farmers were able to harvest plentiful crops of wheat, rice, sugar cane, cotton and indigo, as well as a variety of fruit. Craftsmen in Lahore and Amritsar began to make a reputation for producing silks, shawls, carpets and metal ware, which were exported throughout the region. As Patwant Singh and Jyoti Raj wrote, 'the Sikhs, with their entrepreneurial drive and inclination to spend well and indulge themselves fully, were changing the character of the Punjab.'[ix]

Despite these advances, political power within the Sikh confederacy remained scattered among many fiefdoms, which formed a kind of commonwealth of domains that tended to compete amongst themselves for power and territory, but fought in unison against common non-Sikh enemies. At the end of the eighteenth century a remarkable leader emerged, whose genius was to unite the Punjab's quarrelling warlords and create a Sikh kingdom and then an ever-expanding empire. This was Ranjit Singh, father of Duleep Singh.

Ranjit's name, suitably enough, meant 'victor in battle', but as a child he was not prepossessing: he had lost an eye to smallpox, which also left his skin pockmarked, and he remained small in stature. In every other respect, he grew to be formidable, and while still a teenager he lived up to his name by commanding a Sikh force in a victorious battle against the Afghan army sent to invade the Punjab. In 1799, aged only eighteen, he defeated a second Afghan army, which had occupied Lahore, and took possession of the city. He immediately showed a wisdom that was astounding for his years and was to prove typical of his governing style. His first public act in Lahore was to pay homage at two of the city's mosques, and he issued a proclamation assuring the citizens, who were mostly Muslims, that they would continue to enjoy peace and freedom from molestation. This was accompanied by a warning to his soldiers that looting would be punished by death, a most exceptional and astute decree in an age when looting was not only the norm, but an important part of the reward expected by conquering soldiers of all ranks. In exchange for his submission, he spared the life of his remaining adversary in Lahore, a Sikh chieftain, who had foolishly imprisoned himself in the fort. When Ranjit finally entered the fort, 'trumpets of happiness were blown and kettledrums of victory beaten in every direction.'[x]

Ranjit Singh became the effective ruler of the Lahore region and in 1801, while still twenty-one, he was proclaimed Maharajah of the Punjab. It was the first time the title had been used by a Sikh; Ranjit Singh was thus the first king of the first Sikh kingdom. Prayers were said in all the mosques and temples across his newly unified kingdom. A royal salute was fired from the fort, and the young Maharajah paraded in his pomp through the streets of Lahore, riding on an elephant and showering the crowds of his subjects with gold and silver coins. By taking the title he was assuming sovereignty over the Sikhs as well as the other people who lived within the loosely established boundaries of the Punjab, a position that allowed him to demand both loyalty and tribute from his subjects. 'Within a short time Ranjit Singh convinced the people of Lahore and neighbouring districts that he did not intend to set up a Sikh kingdom but a Punjabi state in which Muslims, Hindus and Sikhs would be equal before the law and enjoy the same privileges and duties.'[xi] In later life he married women from all three major faiths in order to demonstrate his lack of discrimination, or so he said. Asked why he had only one sighted eye, he is supposed to have replied, 'God wanted me to look upon all religions with one eye, which is why he took away the light from the other.'[xii]

As his empire expanded he began to seem more and more menacing to the British East India Company, which had effectively subdued or annexed all the other independent powers in the sub-continent. The two forces confronted each other at the Sutlej river, which formed the border between their respective territories. (The Sutlej is the easternmost tributary of the Indus. It rises in Tibet, and throughout the Punjab area it flows west and south-west, more or less bisecting the modern state of Punjab.)

In 1806 Ranjit Singh avoided a potential clash with the British army by signing a 'Treaty of Amity and Friendship'. Three years later, after indulging in prolonged and convoluted negotiations, he signed a more important treaty with the British, who by then were feeling anxious about possible French invasions through Afghanistan or Persia. The first article of the Treaty of Amritsar, 1809, declared that 'perpetual friendship shall subsist between the British government and the State of Lahore'. It was an expression on the British side of respect for Ranjit Singh's generalship and an implicit acknowledgement that the 'Kingdom of the Sikhs' was a sovereign state, capable of making a bilateral agreement, one kingdom with another, on terms of equality.

This recognition of equality has echoed down the years in Sikh rhetoric, and it can be heard, for example, in a poster used to advertise *The Black Prince* (2017), the film about Duleep Singh's life starring Satinder Sartaaj. Below the title a tagline boldly proclaims, 'Two Kingdoms Collide'. To be realistic one might say that by the time Duleep Singh was deposed the British had not so much collided with the Sikh kingdom, as run it over and left it for dead. But when Ranjit Singh was at the height of his powers, the British did indeed fear a collision with him, and backed off, making a pact of friendship rather than engage in a fight they feared they might lose.

In fact, Ranjit Singh's territorial ambitions lay to the north, and during the years that followed he established an independent and united empire of some thirteen million inhabitants that included the Punjab and the provinces of Kashmir, Jammu and Peshawar, and whose borders extended as far the Khyber Pass and the foothills of the Himalayas.

Ranjit Singh's regime was characterised by tolerance, compromise, and a reluctance to cause offence to any of his subjects on religious grounds. He was open to influences of all sorts, and was never afraid to adopt new ideas. For example, he co-opted several European officers and under their guidance assiduously modernised his army. Having observed British soldiers on the parade ground, he gave orders to have his own soldiers trained in square bashing. His reign was also a golden age for the arts, not least because he was himself an insatiable collector of treasures of every kind, especially gems. In 1813 he added the Koh-i-noor diamond to his collection. (See below, Chapter 4.) Under his benign influence carpet weaving and metalworking, for which the Lahore region had been famous, were revived. Ranjit Singh's court left an impression of 'unrivalled splendour' on everyone who visited it, and foreign visitors were especially impressed by the lavish use of brightly coloured silks, shawls, carpets and gold brocade. Emily Eden, sister of Governor-General Lord Auckland, commented, 'It reduces European magnificence to a very low pitch.'[xiii] Throughout his reign the Maharajah was eager to identify himself with the glories of the Punjab's heritage, and he restored many Mughal monuments, but he also lavished his wealth and energy on restoring and further beautifying the Golden Temple in Amritsar. He arranged for marble paving to be laid round the pool and marble panels inlaid with exuberant and whimsical designs to face the walls of the temple's lower storey. The gold plating on the exterior walls and the dome, which gives the *Harmandir Sahib* (Abode of God) its everyday name and its worldwide fame, was commissioned by Ranjit Singh.

At first sight the Maharajah's appearance did not seem to match the grandeur of his achievements, nor the magnitude of his power. When Emily Eden was first introduced to the Maharajah in 1838 she described him as looking 'exactly like an old mouse with grey whiskers and one eye', but noted that he had only had to lift a finger to obtain instant obedience.[xiv] Before meeting him Lord Auckland asked Ranjit Singh's foreign minister which of the Maharajah's eyes was missing. The minister replied, 'The Maharajah is like the sun and the sun only has one eye. The splendour and luminosity of his single eye is so much that I have never dared to look at his other eye.'[xv] As his many portraits show, it was his left eye that was damaged.

The French traveller Victor Jacquemont, who met him in 1831, described Ranjit Singh as 'an old fox, compared with whom the wiliest of our diplomats is a mere innocent.' Like other Europeans who had dealings with him, Jacquemont found his company exhausting: 'his conversation is a nightmare. He is almost the first inquisitive Indian I have seen, but his curiosity makes up for the apathy of the whole nation. He asked me a hundred thousand questions about India, the English, Europe, Bonaparte, the world in general and the other one, hell and paradise, the soul, God, the devil, and a thousand things beside...'[xvi] The Frenchman recorded that, although he claimed that women 'no longer gave him any more pleasure than the flowers in the garden', he was notorious for shamelessly flaunting his 'vices', and had often been seen in Lahore with a Muslim prostitute on the back of an elephant, 'indulging in the least innocent of sports.'[xvii]

Towards the end of his reign Ranjit Singh signed yet another treaty with the British, the Tripartite Treaty of 1838. Once again the principle of equality was stressed, and it was specified that 'these countries and places [territories guaranteed to Ranjit Singh] are considered to be the property and to form the estate of the Maharajah... They belong to the Maharajah and his posterity from generation to generation.'[xviii] As it turned out, this property did not pass down the Maharajah's 'posterity' by even a single generation.

As with all such occasions, the signing of the treaty was marked with extravagant and protracted hospitality and the exchange of lavish gifts. The Governor-General, then Lord Auckland, arranged for the Maharajah to receive a splendid sword in a golden scabbard and two thoroughbred Cape horses, as well as jewellery. Lord Auckland also gave the Maharajah a miniature portrait of Queen Victoria, a picture hastily produced for the event by his sister, an amateur painter. William Osborne, his secretary, was given the job of delivering his lordship's presents, and he described the ageing Maharajah: 'Cross-legged in a golden chair, dressed in simple white, wearing no ornaments but a single string of enormous pearls round the waist, and the celebrated Koh-y-nur, or mountain of light, on his arm, – (the jewel rivalled, if not surpassed, in brilliancy by the glance of fire which every now and then shot from his single eye as it wandered restlessly round the circle) – sat the lion of Lahore.' The setting was extremely opulent, 'the floor was covered with rich shawl carpets, and a gorgeous shawl canopy, embroidered with gold and precious stones, supported on golden pillars, covered three parts of the hall.' The son of a minister caught Osborne's eye: 'He was magnificently dressed, and almost entirely covered from the waist upwards with strings of pearls, diamonds, emeralds, and rubies.' Ranjit's Singh's manner of dress might have been simple, but his interest in the presents took Osborne by surprise: 'Contrary to the usual native custom, Runjeet [sic] condescended to examine them very minutely, and appeared to count every pearl and jewel before he gave them into the hands of his treasurer.'[xix]

Duleep Singh is said to have remarked, 'I am the son of one of my father's forty-six wives.'[xx] This is probably stretching the term 'wife', though his father certainly had many mistresses, and perhaps as many as twenty wives, women with whom he underwent some kind of marital ceremony. His appetite for sex was notorious, and according to one biography the women in his life 'numbered literally hundreds if the count includes all his wives, concubines and the regiment of Amazons he had created with an eye on both their physical fitness and striking looks.'[xxi] He informed Osborne that he was interested in adding an Englishwoman to his collection of wives. 'I wanted one myself some time ago, and wrote to the government about it, but they did not send me one.' On another occasion, when studying a portrait of Queen Victoria, he paid her a compliment by saying that 'Her Majesty [would] make a very decent Nautch (dancing) girl.'[xxii]

His last wife was Jindan Kaur, whom he married in 1835, and she proved to be the mother of Duleep Singh, though court scandal always maintained that by then Ranjit Singh was incapable of fathering a child. However, he did recognise his seventh son, and in doing so he placed him in line for succession.

In her way Duleep Singh's mother was no less remarkable than his father. Jindan Kaur was the daughter of the kennel-keeper in charge of the royal hounds, who in the louche atmosphere of the court brought his good-looking, sexually precocious daughter to the attention of the Maharajah, teasing him, according to Anita Anand, 'with the prospect of a passion which might rejuvenate his old age.'[xxiii] When the fifty-five-year-old Ranjit Singh married her, she was eighteen, famous for her beauty and, justly or not, notorious for her promiscuity.

In 1838 Jindan Kaur gave birth to her son, Duleep Singh. Nine months later, the Maharajah Ranjit Singh died, leaving political turmoil behind him.

The statue's inscription states that Duleep Singh succeeded his father to the throne, but this was by no means the case, for a period of murderous internecine rivalry followed Ranjit Singh's death, during which his throne was occupied by a sequence of short-lived claimants. While these bloodthirsty events were unfolding, Jindan Kaur kept her small son safe in the countryside, away from the court, though he must have had some sense of what was taking place in the capital. By 1843, following another outbreak of assassinations within the royal family, she was able to make a credible bid for the throne on her son's behalf with the support of the Sikh army. On 18 September 1843, in Lahore, Duleep Singh was proclaimed Maharajah of the Punjab and his father's empire; he was five years old.

The little boy's accession did nothing to calm the court's homicidal turbulence. His mother chose to rule on his behalf with her brother, Jewahir Singh, a man deeply unpopular with the army. Seeking revenge for the murder of one of their own, the army demanded that Jewahir Singh make a public appearance. By way of protecting himself and stressing his royal connection, he rode to the meeting on an elephant carrying the young Duleep Singh beside him. Jindan Kaur followed behind, as the procession made its way through the crowds of soldiers outside the gates of Lahore. Suddenly bugles sounded, drums began to beat and Jewahir Singh's elephant was made to kneel. Duleep Singh was snatched from the howdah, but could not avoid watching as his uncle was shot and killed with a stroke of a sword. The next day, maddened by grief, Jindan Kaur took her son to see his bloody body. She threw herself on her brother's remains and dragged the boy down with her, screaming and tearing out her hair.[xxiv]

Taking advantage of the confused situation in Lahore and the readiness of the various factions to betray one another, the East India Company seized its opportunity, and went to war with the Sikh army in December 1845. The First Anglo-Sikh War lasted until February the following year, but even though the Sikh army fought with a tenacity and courage that deeply impressed the British, it was finally defeated at the Battle of Sobraon, an engagement said to have cost the Sikhs 10,000 dead and injured men.[xxv] Ranjit Singh's old army was effectively broken, and the Sikhs were forced to accept the Treaty of Lahore in March 1846. As a result they lost the lucrative province of Kashmir. Forcing the Punjabi Sikhs to pay indemnities for the war, the British sold the state to Gulab Singh, a Sikh leader whom they recognised as Maharajah of Kashmir and Jammu.

Under the Treaty's terms Duleep Singh remained ruler of the Punjab, with his mother continuing to act as regent. However, the Treaty of Bhyroval, signed in December 1846, enforced an arrangement that suited British interests much better. Claiming to be the Maharajah's protectors, the British 'consented' to govern on his behalf until he reached the age of sixteen, when he would be allowed to resume his throne. His mother was granted a pension and was replaced by a British Resident in Lahore supported by a Council of Regency, with agents in other cities and regions. In effect, the East India Company had seized control of the government.

Jindan Kaur did not submit willingly to these conditions, and it was not long before the newly installed Resident, Henry Lawrence, decided to neutralise this rebellious woman. The Punjab would be 'perfectly tranquil,' he reported, 'if it were not for the perilous passions of the Queen Mother.'[xxvi] The Governor-General was in no doubt what had to be done. 'As guardians of the boy we have the right to separate him at eight years of age,' he wrote.[xxvii] On 14 August 1847 Jindan Kaur was torn from her son and imprisoned in Lahore Fort. As she was hauled away, she begged the Sikh men in the court to come to their senses and fight, not only for her and her son, but for the survival of the Punjab itself. Her cries were not heeded.

She was then moved to a fortress twenty-five miles from the city. Her letters to Lawrence begging for the return of her child make pitiful reading. 'You have been very cruel to me!... You have snatched my son from me... I cannot bear the pain of this separation. Instead you should put me to death... There is no one with my son. He has no sister, no brother. He has no uncles, senior or junior. His father he has lost. To whose care has he been entrusted?'[xxviii]

If Lawrence had qualms concerning this separation of mother and son, they were soothed by the Governor-General's robust insistence on the political expediency of the Maharani's removal. A year later Lawrence was rewarded with a knighthood and replaced. Lord Dalhousie, who became Governor-General in 1848, also saw Jindan Kaur as a rallying point of rebellion and applied still more brutal methods by exiling her from the Punjab to Chunar Fort, hundreds of miles away in the north-western province. As an additional punishment, her jewellery was spitefully confiscated. Her treatment outraged the Sikhs and caused unrest in Lahore. To undermine support for her cause, and discredit her personally, Dalhousie encouraged a campaign of vilification against her, referring to her as 'Messalina of the Punjab' in his dispatches. A year later she escaped from Chunar Fort, disguised as a servant, and travelled through 800 miles of forest to Nepal, where she was given sanctuary, but on condition that she made no attempt to contact her son. The British kept a wary eye on her, but left her to languish helplessly in Kathmandu under the heartless custody of Nepal's ruler. From the moment when her son was torn from her side in 1847, thirteen and a half years were to pass before she saw him again.

The old kingdom of Ranjit Singh, even though significantly reduced, was still one of the few surviving areas of semi-autonomy in India, and therefore a threat to the power of the East India Company. It was not long before the British found an excuse to start the Second

Anglo-Sikh War (1848-49). Once again the Sikh army proved exceedingly difficult to defeat, even though the British were better equipped and deployed in greater numbers. Some battles were indecisive, and were claimed as victories by both sides. The Battle of Chillianwala, for example, which took place in January 1849, was one of the bloodiest fought by the East India Company, and at the end of the day both armies held their positions, causing a great shock to British military prestige. A British observer wrote later that, 'The Sikhs fought like devils, fierce and untamed... Such a mass of men I never set eyes on and plucky as lions: they ran right on the bayonets and struck their assailants when they were transfixed.'[xxix]

Nonetheless, the Sikhs were defeated in the end. The East India Company completed its annexation of the Punjab by imposing the 1849 Treaty of Lahore on its ten-year-old Maharajah. Signed on 29 March in Lahore, the Treaty was a brief and brutal document, and its terms are worth reading in full:

> I. His Highness the Maharajah Duleep Singh shall resign for himself, his heirs, and his successors all right, title, and claim to the sovereignty of the Punjab, or to any sovereign power whatever.
>
> II. All the property of the State, of whatever description and Chapter wheresoever found, shall be confiscated to the Honourable East India Company, in part payment of the debt due by the State of Lahore to the British Government and of the expenses of the war.

III. The gem called the Koh-i-Noor, which was taken from Shah Sooja-ool-moolk by Maharajah Runjeet Singh, shall be surrendered by the Maharajah of Lahore to the Queen of England.

IV. His Highness Duleep Singh shall receive from the Honourable East India Company, for the support of himself, his relatives, and the servants of the State, a pension of not less than four, and not exceeding five, lakhs of Company's rupees per annum.

V. His Highness shall be treated with respect and honour. He shall retain the title of Maharajah Duleep Singh Bahadoor, and he shall continue to receive during his life such portion of the above-named pension as may be allotted to himself personally, provided he shall remain obedient to the British Government, and shall reside at such place as the Governor-General of India may select.

In a word, Duleep Singh was deprived of everything except his title. In less than six years the child had gone from being Maharajah of a great sovereign kingdom to being the owner of an empty title and beneficiary of a pension dependent on his obedience to his conquerors. During his short life he had been given everything and had seen most of it taken away from him: father, mother, uncle and other close relatives, kingdom, property and possessions. The very symbol of his kingdom's power, the Koh-i-noor, had been confiscated – looted – and given to the queen of his conquerors. He was the innocent embodiment of the Sikhs' humiliation, and that is one reason why he retains his symbolic potency.

In the course of 150 years the Sikhs had turned themselves from a religious sect into an identifiable nation with a kingdom to live in and a Maharajah to rule over it. By 1849 the kingdom was less than half a century old, dating from the time when Ranjit Singh had been proclaimed Maharajah of the Punjab in 1801, but it had become a coherent and recognised entity, a state that was capable of defending its borders and was sufficiently powerful to warrant respect by the British. By the same token, this was the cause of its downfall.

In 1849 the Sikhs lost what they had so briefly possessed, their sovereignty, but in the process they also lost much more – their pride. That is the context in which the Duleep Singh memorial must be understood. At first sight, Ranjit Singh might seem a better subject for the statue; after all, he created the sovereignty that 'the Sikh nation aspires to regain', to quote the inscription. But that would be to overlook the special connection that the British Sikhs have with Duleep Singh, for whom it is claimed that he was the first Sikh immigrant.[xxx] Duleep Singh is the emblem of both the lost kingdom of the Punjab and the new Sikh community in Britain, which followed in his footsteps a century later. The British may have appropriated the Sikhs' kingdom in the nineteenth century, but the Sikhs returned the compliment by laying claim to a piece of Britain for themselves in the twentieth century. Duleep Singh remains the figurehead around which the aspirations for a new émigré self-esteem have gathered.

His place in history will always be prestigious, exactly because he was the son of Ranjit Singh; but he will always be famous as well for being the boy who lost his father's throne. Through no fault of his own, it was his luckless destiny to be crowned and deposed before his childhood was over. Indeed, he was punished for his father's success. If his father had not created so formidable and unified a kingdom, founded on a well-trained, modern army, the British would not have found it necessary to dethrone its ruler and destroy its sovereignty.

Duleep Singh's life as Maharajah effectively came to an end at the durbar outside Lahore's famous fort when, in his last act as ruler of the Punjab, he signed the treaty by tracing the initials of his name in English letters. In advance of this ceremony the Governor-General, Lord Dalhousie, had issued a lengthy manifesto justifying the annexation, which was read out in Persian and Hindustani. By turns self-serving, hypocritical, sententious and downright dishonest, his manifesto is a repellent document; it is, nevertheless, perfectly frank about the intentions of the British government: '[the Governor-General] has resolved upon declaring the British sovereignty in the Punjab, and upon the *entire subjection* of the Sikh nation.'[xxxi] (My emphasis.)

On that day in March 1849 Duleep Singh signed away the rest of his life as surely as he signed away his title. Even as an aristocratic spendthrift, rusticated in the backwoods of Norfolk and shooting at nothing more offensive than pheasants, he continued to pay the price for his father's success. For fear that the mere prestige of his lineage would be sufficient to rouse the Punjabis to rebellion, the British authorities made certain that he was forever impotent as a political force. No matter how tearfully Queen Victoria may have wrung her hands over his moral transgressions, no matter how pompously the India Office may have scolded his financial follies, the fact is that his many failures of character suited the purpose of the British government. Duleep Singh in Britain was, as we shall see, a British creation, but to understand the bronze horseman of Thetford we must try to keep in sight the ghost of Ranjit Singh's successor who might have existed if that little boy had not been forced to sign him away in 1849.

Three

SURRENDER COMPLETED

After the Maharajah was deposed, his welfare and destiny fell into the hands of Lord Dalhousie, the Governor-General. He did not regard his young charge with much sympathy. Duleep Singh was, he wrote, 'a child notoriously surreptitious, a brat begotten of a bishti (water carrier), and no more the son of old Runjit Singh than Queen Victoria is.'[xxxii] On another occasion he wrote, 'I am sorry for him, poor little fellow, although it is superfluous compassion ... he will have a good and regular stipend, ("without income tax") all his life, and will die in his bed like a gentleman; which under other circumstances, he certainly would not have done.'[xxxiii] His prophecy was not altogether fulfilled, though the idea of his being redeemed from his Indian patrimony by being converted into British gentleman was the template for his upbringing that most officials shared.

The official chosen to be Duleep Singh's new 'Superintendent' was Dr John Login, a Scottish doctor who recommended himself to the authorities because he was efficient and punctiliously honest. Login was appointed Governor of the citadel of Lahore, a post that made him responsible for the royal treasure, the Koh-i-noor, and the Maharajah. In this one respect Duleep Singh was fortunate: as his guardian, Login proved both conscientious and affectionate, and he was supported by his wife, Lena, whose feelings for the boy were no less tender. This couple were to be his substitute parents until he reached adulthood.

In 1890, when Duleep Singh was still alive, though living in exile in Paris, Lady Login published her memoirs of the years when her husband, who died in 1863, had been Duleep Singh's guardian. With wifely modesty she called her book *Sir John Login and Duleep Singh*.[xxxiv] Covering much the same ground, but adding more material about herself and her family, she later wrote a second book of memoirs, published in 1916, under the more assertive title, *Lady Login's Recollections: Court Life and Camp Life 1820-1904*.[xxxv] Both these books, but especially the first, offer an indispensable source of information about Duleep Singh's childhood and adolescence; indeed, they are virtually the only source available in English.

Lady Login was on hand to witness in person many of the chief events of the Maharajah's life, and as a memoirist she made an excellent raconteur with a good eye for the telling or colourful detail. She was able to quote liberally from her husband's correspondence with his colleagues, including the reliably caustic Lord Dalhousie, and she had access to official documents of the period, from which she selected lengthy extracts. As a result her first book is a virtual archive of the whole period of her husband's guardianship.

Because of her unique position in relation to Duleep Singh, and because of the absence of alternative records, we have no choice but to take her word for what happened. No doubt she did her best to present a fair and kindly record, but the fact remains that, despite her well-meaning intentions, her point of view was decidedly partial: after all, she was the loyal wife of a British civil servant who was charged with the ultimate task of ensuring that the unseated Maharajah posed no threat to the imperial regime. It is in that light that we must read her books, especially her account of certain key moments during Duleep Singh's upbringing at her husband's hands.

From the outset Login believed that Duleep Singh should be sent to England to complete his education and 'not [be] left to grow up idle and debauched in India, with nothing to do'. Writing to his wife, Login said, 'He will surely have as much to live on as any of our nobles, considering what *he* has lost and *we* gained! Why, then, should he not be brought up to the life of one? (in the highest sense of the word) – he is young enough to mould.'[xxxvi]

Dalhousie was of a different opinion and in 1850 decreed that the twelve-year-old Maharajah and his household should be deported to Fatehgarh, a small cantonment town in Uttar Pradesh, 400 miles distant from Lahore. Here Duleep Singh presided in relative luxury over a kind of nursery court in exile, attended by a large retinue of servants and supervised by the Logins. The picture Lady Login paints of what were to be Duleep Singh's last years of residence in India have a sunny quality. If she is to be believed, his mentors did not have to exert themselves unduly in anglicising him: he did the job for them voluntarily, slowly shedding his connections with his family, religion, language and culture.

The Governor-General made it clear that he 'did not wish to countenance any relations henceforth between the Maharajah and the Sikhs, whether by alliance with a Sikh family [through marriage], or sympathy with Sikh feeling.'[xxxvii] In the event, Duleep Singh made this wish easy for Login to realise. When arranging for their departure to Fatehgarh, Login left it to Duleep Singh to choose the staff that would accompany him. It appears to have been a calculated gesture, because 'as I had foreseen' the boy 'detached' a great many Sikhs from his retinue, and appointed Muslims in their stead. He left Lahore without taking with him a copy of the Granth (Sikh holy book), and the family priest in charge of his religious education was not a Sikh, but a Brahmin (Hindu) *porohut* or family priest.[xxxviii]

Duleep Singh confided in Login that since the assassination of his uncle, he had 'entertained a dread of his own countrymen, and a dislike to their religion and all connected with them.' Login reported that the Maharajah's religious education had been neglected, and he suspected that his disbelief concerning the Sikh legends that were read to him was not discouraged by his favourite attendant, a Muslim. The result was predictable. While his prejudices against his own people and their faith were gaining strength, 'circumstances had occurred in his outward position to lead him to consider the English his most sincere friends.'[xxxix]

At that time Duleep Singh's mother was in Nepal, but Login reported to Dalhousie that as far as he could judge 'not the least desire exists on the part of the Maharajah to communicate with his mother.'[xl] Indeed, he appeared to dislike any reference to her, and never mentioned her name himself. He told Login that he had heard nothing of his mother since she had left Lahore and that she had dishonoured him. Was she not kind to him? Login asked. No, she used to strike him daily! Apparently, the boy had come across an allusion in a history book of 'his being the acknowledged, though not the reputed, son of Ranjit Singh', and Login commented that her reputation and behaviour tended to confirm rumours about his dubious paternity. The Maharajah agreed, and told Login that 'he had frequently made up his mind, while at Lahore, that he should have his mother killed, that she might not disgrace him!'[xli]

While in Fatehgarh the boy enjoyed the privileges of his rank and pursued his favourite activity, hunting with hawks or his pack of greyhounds. At the same time he began to identify more and more closely with England and the culture of his captors: he repeatedly asked to be allowed to travel to England; he preferred English friends to those of his own race; he read books about life in England; he forsook Hindustani (Urdu) in favour of English and soon spoke it fluently with a 'good' accent.

Towards the end of 1851 he told Login that he wished to demonstrate that he was no longer a Sikh by cutting off his long hair, which he wore 'twisted up into a ball above the brow, and covered with the bright coloured under-turban'. He thought it would make him look more like his English friends. Login wisely urged him to defer for at least twelve months, but in the end he was given permission to make this definitive gesture of separation from his old faith. He brought his tress of hair and gave it to Lady Login as 'a memento'; she wrote that it was 'long and abundant as a woman's'.[xlii]

As his education proceeded he also expressed an eager desire to embrace Christianity. It was a delicate matter. With his eye on this world rather than the next, Dalhousie immediately understood the benefit of conversion by 'his little friend'. 'Politically,' he wrote to a colleague, 'we could desire nothing better, for it destroys his possible influence forever.' On the other hand, he was worried that the government might be accused of 'tampering with the mind of a child',[xliii] and so he instructed that the Maharajah's baptism should be delayed. However, Login reported that the boy 'continued inflexible in his resolve', surprising his tutors. In most branches of education his natural disposition was 'to shirk anything in the shape of steady application' and he often fell asleep among his books but when it came to religion he 'never tired of the restraints of study'.[xliv]

As a reward for his application, the Maharajah was finally baptised in 1853. Dalhousie wrote to him, saying that he thanked God for putting into his heart the truth of 'our' holy religion, and that he hoped 'you may show to your countrymen in India an example of a pure and blameless life, as befits a Christian prince.'[xlv] 'Pure and blameless' were of course attributes of a prince who was both devout and politically submissive.

(Many years later, in 1884, Duleep Singh circulated a book entitled *The Maharajah Duleep Singh and the Government*, which included an autobiographical section. For what it is worth, when describing his conversion to Christianity at Fatehgarh, he added the assurance that 'young as he was, the choice was his own.'[xlvi])

Dalhousie recognised that the Maharajah's eagerness to exile himself in England and turn his back on his Punjabi heritage was highly convenient to the Indian government, which continued to fear that he might become a figurehead, if not an active leader, in a movement to overthrow British rule. In 1854, when Duleep Singh was fifteen, permission was finally given for him to travel to England, but Dalhousie, who always saw these matters with cold-blooded clarity, advised his tutor Login, to 'press upon his Highness that while in India he receives all the honours of his rank – in England he will be entitled only to courtesy.'[xlvii]

As a parting gift Dalhousie gave Duleep Singh a Bible, saying that he hoped it might occasionally remind the Maharajah of him. He added that ever since he had been made responsible for Duleep Singh as a little boy he had regarded him 'in some sort as my son'. The Bible, he explained, was the volume he would offer to his own child, 'as the best of all gifts, since in it alone is to be found the secret of real happiness either in this world or in that which is to come.'[xlviii] (Dalhousie's gift can be seen in the Ancient House Museum, Thetford.)

The Maharajah and his party set sail for England on 19 April 1854. In Cairo arrangements were made for him to stay for a while and extend his education by seeing something of the sights. He was taken to the Pyramids, where he conducted a race to the top of one of them, to the annoyance of his guides. He was also taken to the American Mission in Cairo, a fateful visit, as it turned out. The United Presbyterian Church of North America had opened a series of schools with the hope of converting Coptic Christians to Protestantism, and Lady Login reported that the Maharajah was 'greatly interested to see so many orphan girls being educated in the Christian religion'.[xlix] Continuing his voyage, the Maharajah was very pleased to note that in Malta and then Gibraltar his arrival was acknowledged by a salute of twenty-one guns, as befitted his royal status. He docked in Southampton in May 1854.

On the eve of the Maharajah's departure, Dalhousie had written to a friend in England, saying, 'He is at an awkward age, and has dark callow all over his face, but his manners are apparently nice and gentlemanlike, and he now speaks English exceedingly well... I earnestly desire this boy should make a good impression in England, and equally so that he should not be spoiled and made a fool of.'[l] Dalhousie was therefore gratified to receive reports that the Maharajah, having landed in England, had pleased everyone with his 'unassuming manners and well-bred bearing.'[li]

However, beyond hoping that he would be well behaved, neither Dalhousie nor Login seemed to have envisaged any kind of role in England for their young man beyond that of harmless prince-in-exile. It was a destiny that he fulfilled, but at tragic cost to himself and those attached to him.

Among the many appointed and self-appointed parental figures in Duleep Singh's life was Queen Victoria herself. As soon as Duleep Singh had arrived in England she gave him an audience. Lady Login reports that he came away charmed with 'the kindness of her manner to him', and that every successive meeting added to the warmth of his feelings for both the Queen and Prince Albert.[lii] This warmth was mutual. In a remarkably succinct and articulate letter to Dalhousie, the Queen summed up her emotions in relation to the fifteen-year-old Duleep Singh, emotions that were to prevail, despite many challenges, throughout their long mutual acquaintance. 'It is not without mixed feelings of pain and sympathy,' she wrote, 'that the Queen sees the young Prince, once destined to so high and powerful a position, and now reduced to so dependent a one by her arms; his youth, amiable character, and striking good looks, as well as being a Christian, the first of his high rank who has embraced our faith, must incline every one favourably towards him, and it will be a pleasure to us to do all we can to be of use to him and to befriend and protect him.'[liii]

The Queen was so impressed with him that she decreed that he was to be treated as equal in rank to a European prince, and that as chief of the princes of India he should take precedence after the royal family.[liv] He was frequently invited to Windsor and Osborne, and he was encouraged to make friends with the royal princes. Needless to say, Dalhousie was not impressed. In a letter to his friend Sir George Couper, he spelt out the reality of the Maharajah's situation with his customary scorn: 'I am a little afraid that this exceeding distinction will not be for his future comfort. If he is to live and die in England, good and well, but if he is to return to India, he is not likely to be rendered more contented with his position there by being so highly treated in England. After breakfasting with queens and princesses, I doubt his much liking the necessity of leaving his shoes at the door of the Governor-General's room, when he is admitted to visit him which he will certainly be again required to do.'[lv]

Happily infatuated with her new favourite, the Queen commissioned her favourite court painter, the German artist Franz Xaver Winterhalter, to paint Duleep Singh's portrait, offering him a fee of £300.[lvi]

Winterhalter had established an incontestable position as Europe's specialist painter of royal and aristocratic portraiture. He was cherished for his ability to create likenesses of his illustrious subjects that invested them with a lively immediacy, but did not compromise their all-important dignity. He was especially adept at using rich fabrics and vivid colours to suggest a kind of lush but respectable sensuality in his female subjects. Winterhalter first came to England in 1842, returning several times to paint Victoria and then her family. His portraits of the Queen as a young woman have a special tenderness that perhaps explains her liking for his work.

Duleep Singh sat for Winterhalter in the White Drawing Room at Buckingham Palace, and the Queen attended several of the sittings. She noted in her journal on 10 July 1854 that her pet painter ('our dear Winterhalter') was 'in ecstasies at the beauty and nobility of bearing of the young Maharajah.'[lvii] 'He was very amiable and patient, standing so still and giving a sitting of upwards of 2 hrs.'[lviii] Lady Login concurred: he was 'a very handsome youth, slight and graceful.'[lix]

Winterhalter stood the Maharajah on a dais, where he posed in full princely costume. Lady Login tells us that the painter, 'wishing the picture to be a permanent portrait of the young Oriental prince in his full dress, has given to the sitter the height he judged he would attain when he reached manhood.'[lx] In the event, the young prince never did achieve the slender stature that Winterhalter anticipated on his behalf. Nor was this the portrait's only distortion.

As a painter renowned for his sumptuous handling of fabrics, Winterhalter made the most of the Maharajah's costume by lovingly reproducing its opulent textiles, its numerous jewels and thick braiding. Duleep Singh is portrayed in lemon, tight-fitting silk trousers and golden slippers with curled toes that echo the yellow stripes in his turban, which is decorated with jewels and topped with a silver aigrette and diamond star. Wrapped round his hips is what appears to be an enormous cream-coloured shawl made of some rich material into which is woven a complex pattern in coral pink. It hangs in extravagant folds that droop nearly to the ground. Around his waist is another shawl, woven in stripes of emerald and white; some of this material is folded over his left arm. His left hand grips an elaborately worked sword belt that is slung over his shoulder, its surface crusted with braided gold. He wears a white silk tunic woven with amber stripes, whose collar and cuffs are heavily trimmed with pearls. Golden hoops hang from his ears, and from them depend jewelled droplets. A rope of pearls is wound several times round his neck, and attached to its lowest strand is the miniature portrait of the Queen, which Lord Auckland had presented to his father.

Duleep Singh stands with one slippered foot turned at right angles to the other in a stance that is almost balletic and seems at odds with the martial note struck by the sheathed sword, an essential Sikh symbol, on which his right hand rests. He appears to be looking down at us, an illusion designed to exaggerate the height he would never attain. His expression is solemn, a little wistful; he is undeniably handsome, his features not yet enveloped in the flesh that accumulated round his jowls in later life. As noted by Dalhousie, his chin and cheeks are outlined by a strip of beard and his lip carries a fledgling moustache. He cuts a regal figure, but to British eyes, unaccustomed to the profligate excesses in which Indian rulers wrapped themselves (not, however, Ranjit Singh), the picture must have represented a young man whose manliness was compromised by the confection of colours and materials in which he was swathed. He was the very essence of the Oriental, as imagined by the Queen: exotic but decadent, beautiful but as innocuous as a tiger skin. (Her romantic vision of India was to be soured by the savagery that sprang from the depths of British nightmares during the so-called Mutiny three years later.)

The turban is the defining feature of the portrait, the part of his costume that unmistakably identified him as a Sikh. It is an ornate and lavish piece of headgear, comprising two separate pieces of cloth: the red *paggari* that underlies the turban proper and is visible in a swathe across his forehead, and the striped gold and light-blue cloth with silver fringes that wraps his head and encloses his ears in its many layers. The turban's peak is ornamented with jewels: a diamond aigrette and star attached to a peacock feather, and beside it a dangling cluster of jewels called the *jigha*. (These turban decorations were symbols of royalty, once popularised by the Mughals and appropriated later by the Sikh rulers.[lxi])

The Queen had reservations about his turban when she first met him: 'His young face is indeed beautiful & one regrets that his peculiar headdress hides so much of it.'[lxii] Lord Dalhousie took a more worldly view: 'The "night-cappy" appearance of his turban is his strongest national feature. Do away with that and he has no longer any outward and visible sign of a Sikh about him.'[lxiii] In any case it was an empty symbol, because as we have seen he had already cut off his long hair, and his turban contained neither his uncut hair, nor, presumably, the kangha (comb) that committed Sikhs carry with them at all times.

Despite the impression of material solidity conveyed by the Maharajah's costume, the 'ground' on which he stands is generalised and characterless, a kind of no-man's-land. All attention is directed to the figure and his colourful wardrobe, while he appears to occupy an almost abstract space. The immediate patch where he stands seems sandy, but the surrounding landscape is flat and faintly green, receding into a featureless, hazy distance. This is not a topography so much as an absence of imagination. Winterhalter had never been to the Punjab, and was apparently disinclined to borrow from the many paintings of Indian landscape that must have been available to him. Brian Keith Axel describes this void as a 'homogenous, nondescript platform of a stage', and argues that it represents a problem that Winterhalter failed to solve: the manner of the painting would have been suitable for a wealthy, powerful subject, but Duleep Singh was a king without a kingdom, since the literal ground on which he used to stand had become colonial property.[lxiv] A deliberately political portrait, underlining the young man's alienation from his home and erstwhile possessions, would have been quite unacceptable to Victoria, even if Winterhalter had thought along those lines. Nonetheless, the portrait has an eerie quality, as if the subject were a fancy-dress character in search of a play, which, indeed, was the case. For Axel the portrait 'redoubles' Duleep Singh's surrender.[lxv]

And yet the landscape is not altogether vacant. Discreetly sketched in the faraway background, as if hovering on the horizon, can be seen a cluster of white domes and towers gleaming in the milky sky, which are recognisable as the entrance to the fort at Lahore. They appear in a drawing of Lahore which Winterhalter may have seen while he was at work on the portrait. The Queen recorded in her journal that she showed the Maharajah a 'view of Lahore done by young Hardinge.'[lxvi] This was the eldest son of Sir Henry Hardinge, the Governor-General (1844-48) who had defeated the Sikhs in the First Anglo-Sikh War. 'Young' Hardinge's picture shows the procession of elephants that carried the seven-year-old Duleep Singh towards his palace in Lahore after making his formal submission to his father in 1846. Perhaps this was 'the view' that Victoria showed to Duleep Singh while he sat for his portrait, and perhaps Winterhalter looked over his shoulder at that moment and took a mental note. If so, Winterhalter's landscape, far from being 'nondescript', was a specific location, the scene of Duleep Singh's first, official humiliation.

The Winterhalter portrait was commissioned by the Queen herself and was hung in the Princesses' Corridor in Buckingham Palace as part of her private collection.[lxvii] It would be interesting to know the instructions she gave Winterhalter when commissioning him. Whatever they were, it seems she was pleased with the result, perhaps because it reassured her that anxieties concerning Duleep Singh's sense of self-worth were misplaced. He might have lost his kingdom, but the picture showed that the charitable and understanding British had left him with sufficient pride and affluence to preserve his royal dignity. He might no longer have a throne to sit on, but he had not been deprived of his royal aura; though powerless, he had retained the prestige of a prince. Throughout Duleep Singh's life, it was always a matter of great concern to the Queen that due deference was paid to his rank, and that he was equipped with the means to support himself in a style befitting the equivalent of a senior British aristocrat. In these matters she always showed him a special sympathy, as one monarch to another.

Duleep Singh was painted, sketched and photographed many times during his life, but no image was reproduced more frequently than the portrait made by Franz Xaver Winterhalter in 1854, and none did more to establish his image in Britain: exotic, a little effeminate, glamorous, colourful; in a word, ornamental. Surely, this is an image to be proud of? After all, it was commissioned by Queen Victoria as a sign of her high regard and friendship; it has remained on display in royal households ever since it was painted; it shows a prince in the full splendour of royalty. But, as I have tried to show, it can also be read as a portrait of his abjectness; it looks magnificent, but in its way it is a depiction of surrender.

Four
KOH-I-NOOR

IT WAS AT THIS TIME THAT THE KOH-I-NOOR DIAMOND,

LATER TO BE INCORPORATED INTO THE CROWN JEWELS, PASSED TO THE BRITISH AUTHORITIES.

(From the inscription on the plinth of Duleep Singh's statue in Thetford)

While Duleep Singh was posing for the Winterhalter portrait 'a most interesting episode' took place. 'Tell me, Lady Login,' the Queen enquired, 'does the Maharajah ever mention the Koh-i-noor? Does he seem to regret it, and would he like to see it again? Find out for me before the next sitting, and mind you let me know *exactly* what he says.'[lxviii] The famous diamond had been transferred from the Maharajah's treasury to the Queen's collection in London under the terms of the Treaty of Lahore in 1849, but she had not yet worn it in public, and now that the Maharajah himself was in England, she 'had a delicacy about doing so' in his presence, as she confided in Lady Login.[lxix]

Lady Login continues: 'Little did Her Majesty guess the perturbation into which her command threw a loyal subject! … there was no other subject that so filled the thoughts and conversation of the Maharajah, his relatives and dependents! For the confiscation of the jewel which to the Oriental is the symbol of the sovereignty of India, rankled in his mind even more than the loss of his kingdom.'[lxx]

The legendary Koh-i-noor, known as the Mountain of Light, having passed through many hands during its long history, was acquired by Shah Shuja when he became the King of Afghanistan in 1803.[lxxi] Weighing a stupendous 190.3 metric carats, it had the reputation of being the most valuable diamond in the world; it was certainly the most highly prized. A sixteenth-century assessor poetically calculated its worth as the cost of feeding the entire world for two and a half days.[lxxii]

Shuja's possession of this treasure proved to be short-lived. In 1809 he was deposed, though he managed to hide the diamond and retain it. After a period of ignominious wandering in exile, he was imprisoned in Kashmir. By then the diamond was in the safekeeping of his wife, the resourceful Wa'fa Begum, who had taken refuge in Lahore, where she was at the mercy of Ranjit Singh. Knowing that the Maharajah was eager to get his hands on the diamond, she persuaded him to rescue Shuja by offering to give him the Koh-i-noor in return for the favour. Ranjit Singh sent an expedition to Kashmir in 1813. Shuja was released from his dungeon and brought to Lahore, but he proved reluctant to keep his side of the bargain his wife had struck. Ranjit Singh put him under house arrest, restricted his rations, separated him from his harem and confined him in a cage. According to Shuja's own account, which is disputed, he did not finally yield up the diamond until his son was tortured in front of his eyes.[lxxiii]

Seeking reassurance from Wa'fa Begum, Ranjit Singh asked her to estimate the value of his new treasure. 'Take five strong men,' she told him. 'Let the first throw a stone northward, the second eastward, the third southward, the fourth westward, and the fifth upward. Fill the space thus outlined with gold and you still will not have achieved the value of the Mountain of Light.'[lxxiv] Unlike many Indian princes, Ranjit Singh was celebrated for the simplicity of his dress, but once the Koh-i-noor was in his possession, he took to wearing it on his arm, a conspicuous reminder, for anyone who doubted it, of his unchallengeable power.

Thus, the Koh-i-noor, following its barbarous change of ownership, came into the possession of the Sikhs, where it would remain for only thirty-six years. It was not a trivial acquisition; indeed, according to William Dalrymple, 'it would become in many ways a symbol of their sovereignty', an assessment that Lady Login had also made.[lxxv] However, there was something to be learnt about the precarious nature of this sovereignty from the fact that it was symbolised by a diamond with an ominously erratic history of tenure.

After his father's death the notorious gem remained in the royal treasury, and Duleep Singh inherited it when he assumed his father's throne in 1843. Six years later, when the British defeated the Sikhs in the Second Anglo-Sikh War, they seized everything in the treasury, including the Koh-i-noor and Ranjit Singh's golden throne, now in the Victoria and Albert Museum. The importance of the Koh-i-noor, both as an object and a symbol, is demonstrated by the separate clause allocated to the jewel in the 1849 Treaty of Lahore, one of only five clauses in that terse document.

Article II decreed that all state property was to be confiscated to the East India Company as part payment for the recent war, but the Koh-i-noor was singled out for different treatment. Article III stated that 'The gem called the Koh-i-noor ... shall be *surrendered* by the Maharajah of Lahore to the Queen of England.' (My emphasis.)

During the Second Anglo-Sikh War, Dalhousie had written, 'The task before me is the utter destruction and prostration of the Sikh power. The subversion of its dynasty and the subjection of its people. This must be done promptly, fully and finally.'[lxxvi] It was in the same spirit that he prosecuted the peace. As we have seen, the Treaty of Lahore was a comprehensive demolition of power. The boy-maharajah was stripped of everything he had inherited, especially his claim to the sovereignty of the Punjab. Furthermore, he was obliged to surrender the very symbol of that sovereignty.

The Koh-i-noor was duly shipped to England and presented to the Queen. Dalhousie, who as Governor-General had ratified the 1849 treaty, was in no doubt as to the significance of this royal acquisition. The diamond's surrender did not please the East India Company, which would have preferred to have presented it as a gift to the Queen, but Dalhousie was clear that the stone was a spoil of war and should be treated accordingly. Writing to a friend in August 1849, he acknowledged that the East India Company was 'ruffled', but his motive was simply this: 'that it was more for the honour of the Queen that the Koh-i-noor should be surrendered directly from the hand of the conquered prince into the hands of the sovereign who was his conqueror, than it should be presented to her as a gift – which is always a favour – by any joint-stock company among her subjects.'[lxxvii]

Sir John Hobhouse, President of the Board of Control of the East India Company, disagreed with his colleagues and fully understood the real meaning of the diamond's surrender: 'If it is to be regarded as booty, it is clearly the Queen's and not the Company's; and I do not see how anything acquired by force of arms, or, in other words, by the conquest of the Punjab, can be considered in any other light than that of prize of war.'[lxxviii]

We must remind ourselves of the wording on the statue's inscription that relates to the Koh-i-noor. It reads: 'It was at this time [1849] that the Koh-I-Noor diamond, later to be incorporated into the crown jewels, *passed to the British*.' (My emphasis.) The fact was that, so far from 'passing', it had been confiscated from its rightful owner, then a child. Furthermore, Duleep Singh's surrender of the diamond was understood by the officials in charge to be a gesture of subjugation that the conquered was forced to make to his conqueror. The Koh-i-noor did not 'pass to the British'; it was surrendered to the Queen herself, a very different matter. Duleep Singh was made to deliver up both his nation's sovereignty and its symbol.

Following its safe transfer from Lahore to London the Koh-i-noor was put on display in 1851 at the Great Exhibition, where it was exhibited in its own special case, a gilded iron cage surmounted by a replica of the British crown – an inadvertent symbol of Duleep Singh's own situation.

The Times called it 'the Lion' of the exhibition, and it proved to be an object of great curiosity. Special security measures designed by Chubb, the famous safe-maker, had to be put in place, with a policeman stationed at either end of its gallery. The gem was placed on a device that caused it, on the slightest touch, to retreat into an iron box. A dozen little gas jets were arranged round it with the idea that their flames would be reflected in its sparkling facets. However, the crowds were disappointed. Notwithstanding its great size, the captive diamond refused to scintillate. Things were not improved by the intolerable heat generated by the gas jets inside the special cabin where it was displayed, but the press began to blame the gem itself, as if it were churlishly refusing to perform for the British public. 'There appears to be something impracticable about the gem,' reported the *Standard* in a mood of sour disappointment, 'for the more it is lighted up, the less it is disposed to display its splendour.'[lxxix]

As a result, Prince Albert decided that, with the consent of the government, the diamond should be cut and polished once the Great Exhibition closed. The procedure was supervised by Prince Albert and the Duke of Wellington, who was eager to take a hand in the cutting, and after thirty-eight days' work the Mountain of Light had been reduced in weight by about forty-two per cent. Now it sparkled, but instead of weighing 190.3 metric carats, as it had done when Ranjit Singh wore it on his arm, it was diminished by more than half to its current 93 metric carats. Originally, it had been more or less egg-shaped, but now it was flatter and rounder, having been cut into an 'oval stellar brilliant' in a perfectly symmetrical design, with thirty-three facets on its upper side and thirty-three underneath. Prince Albert footed the bill, which amounted to a staggering £8,000.[lxxx]

This was the diamond that Victoria wondered if Duleep Singh would like to see while Winterhalter was at work in Buckingham Palace. Lady Login followed her instructions and picked a suitable moment to ask the Maharajah. He replied with an emphatic yes: 'I would give a good deal to hold it again in my own hand ... because I was but a child, an infant, when forced to surrender it by treaty; but now that I am a man, I should like to have it in my power to place it myself in her [the Queen's] hand.'

Lady Login regarded this as 'a charming and chivalrous sentiment'.[lxxxi] (It is interesting to note from this anecdote that neither Duleep Singh nor Lady Login were in any doubt as to the true nature of the exchange of ownership: it had been a matter of 'surrender'.)

The next day, while Duleep Singh posed for Winterhalter on a dais, Lady Login was able to report favourably to the Queen, who, after consultation with Albert, despatched a gentleman-in-waiting to the Tower of London. Half an hour later a group of beefeaters in their 'gorgeous uniforms' appeared at the door, escorting an official who carried a small casket. The Queen said, 'Maharajah, I have something to show you!' Duleep Singh jumped down and the Queen put the diamond in his hand. He took it to the window to examine it closely, turning it over and over. The Queen watched 'with sympathy not unmixed with anxiety'. For Lady Login it was the 'most excruciating uncomfortable quarter of an hour' she had ever passed. An awful terror seized her, for she feared that she had unwittingly deceived the Queen now that she saw the Maharajah holding the stone in his hand 'as if unable to part with it again, now he had it once more in his possession!' She wondered if in a fit of madness he might fling 'the precious talisman' out of the window. But with a deep sigh, 'as if summoning up his resolution after a profound struggle', the Maharajah walked over to the Queen. With 'a deferential reverence' he placed the diamond in her hands, saying, 'It is for me, Ma'am, the greatest pleasure thus to have the opportunity, as a loyal subject, of *myself* tendering to *my Sovereign* the Koh-i-noor!'[lxxxii] (Emphases in the original.) Then he quietly resumed his place on the dais, and Winterhalter got back to work.

This extraordinary scene – Queen, Consort, Maharajah, Winterhalter, Lady Login, assorted ladies- and gentlemen-in-waiting, gorgeously uniformed beefeaters, officials, the glittering diamond in its casket – represents a key moment in Duleep Singh's biography, and his mentality is difficult to read. It is worth remembering that he had not yet turned sixteen.

His little speech, assuming Lady Login reported it accurately, was a graceful response to a delicate situation, but it was also ambiguous. Was he trying to ingratiate himself to Victoria, the new mother-figure in his life? Was he trying to recover a little self-esteem by suggesting that in some mysterious way the diamond was still in his gift and therefore his, as 'a loyal subject', to give to his queen? Was he trying to confer dignity on what had been an act of larceny by presenting himself, not as a helpless victim, but as a prince who retained the right to dispose of his belongings as he chose?

When Dalhousie heard about the 'interesting episode', his reaction was scathing. In a letter to a friend he wrote that the idea of the Koh-i-noor's being a present from Duleep to the Queen was 'arrant humbug'. Duleep Singh 'knew as well as I did it was nothing of the sort; and if I had been within a thousand miles of him he would not have dared to utter such a piece of trickery.' He went on to suggest that Victoria had been bewitched by his beautiful eyes, 'splendid orbs' he had inherited from his mother.[lxxxiii]

Thirty years later, in 1884, Duleep Singh compiled and issued for private circulation his account of his treatment at the hands of the British authorities, *Maharajah Duleep Singh and the Government*. He arranged for it to be bound in leather and distributed among people he considered to be influential, which included the Queen, Lady Login and senior figures at the India Office. It was an embittered document by a man who had good cause to be bitter, but whose incurable extravagance had lost him the sympathy that his dethronement had won for him as a child. When not spending money, Duleep Singh spent much of his adult life trying to win justice in the matter of the British government's stewardship of his wealth. In his book he argued that, despite their treaty obligations, the 'distinguished and accomplished persons' who had constituted the British rulers of the Punjab had simply appropriated the estates and property that rightfully belonged to him. Summing up his position in a single sentence in his conclusion, he wrote, 'The whole [his estates and property] has been treated as if it had been a spoil of war.'[lxxxiv]

However, on the subject of the Koh-i-noor the Maharajah made some comments that may seem surprising in the light of the injustice that, he claimed, had pervaded all his dealings with the British. Repeating the sentiments he expressed all those years ago as a fifteen-year-old, he wrote that 'the Maharajah feels it an honour' to have bestowed the diamond on the Queen. 'So far from regretting its loss, he would be glad to have it again in his power freely to offer it for Her Majesty's gracious acceptance.' And his reason for saying so? 'He considers that the Koh-i-noor should belong to the ruling power in India.'[lxxxv]

Perhaps the wording of the inscription should be read in this light. At first sight, the word 'passed' seems to be an insipid euphemism for surrender or looting, but the word 'pass' does at least preserve the more nuanced possibility that the diamond, despite Dalhousie's ferocity when it came to disempowering Duleep Singh, was still the Maharajah's to dispose of as a matter of natural justice. Rising above the circumstances of his dethronement and exile, the fifteen-year-old Duleep Singh had, in his own words, *tendered* the Koh-i-noor *himself* to his *sovereign*. He had chosen his words with care.

The Koh-i-noor was said to be cursed, though like many curses its terms were ambivalent: its owner was granted the power and right to rule the world, but would meet with death and misfortune; at the same time, the curse excluded any woman who wore it. Whether out of superstition, or care for Duleep Singh's feelings, or embarrassment concerning its provenance, Victoria never incorporated the Koh-i-noor in her crown. However, she did arrange to have it mounted on a tiara, where it was the centrepiece among 2,000 smaller diamonds.

Part of her reservation may have come from the fact that, without putting too fine a point on it, the diamond had been looted. Of course, looting was so commonplace, especially in India, that this example may have seemed a respectable, even legitimate version of it, undeserving of the vulgar term 'loot'. After all, its removal from the boy, Duleep Singh, had served a political and military symbolic purpose; it was not as if the East India Company had taken the thing out of sheer greed or acquisitiveness. But that in itself may well have caused Her Majesty embarrassment or unease. The thought of wearing a jewel that was not only a conspicuous object of wealth, but a famous symbol of dispossession may have given her pause. 'I always feel so much for these poor deposed Indian Princes,' she wrote in her journal in 1854.[lxxxvi]

There seems to be small point in discussing the legitimacy or otherwise of the Koh-i-noor's removal from the Punjab. It was a commonplace of war in every century before the twentieth that the losing side would be stripped of its valuables as well as its territory; plunder was the reward of victory, the price of defeat. There was no protection in law or convention. As Tiffany Jenkins explained in her book, *Keeping Their Marbles*, taking plunder was not looting, but legal seizure. With reference to Napoleon's methodical pillaging, she wrote, 'It did not violate international law, as the legality of taking works depended on the right of conquest; thus, it was already a standard part of military conquest and part of the common law of warfare.' As Dalhousie was to do in India,

'Napoleon signed treaties with the defeated, specifying the cession of works of art. Sometimes the list documented every single painting, sculpture, and artefact.'[lxxxvii]

The right of conquest was not abandoned as an accepted principle of international law until after the Second World War, when cultural treasures finally received protection under the Hague Convention of 1954, which was designed to safeguard cultural property against looting and the effects of armed conflict.[lxxxviii] The looting of Duleep Singh's treasury was only a fractional part of the great looting of India conducted by the British during its 200-year raid. As Shashi Tharoor points out in his splendid polemic, *Inglorious Empire: What the British Did to India* (a title that encapsulates his thesis), the British methodically stripped India of its enormous wealth. At the beginning of the eighteenth century India's share of the world economy was twenty-three per cent, as large as all of Europe put together. By the time the British hauled down their flag in 1947 it had dropped to three per cent. 'The reason was simple,' Tharour wrote, 'India was governed for the benefit of Britain. Britain's rise for 200 years was financed by its depredations in India.'[lxxxix] Would Dalhousie, for one, have been embarrassed by these statistics? After all, what else was the point of India?

Subsequent monarchs did not share Victoria's inhibitions about displaying the Koh-i-noor in public. After her death, the diamond was set in the crown of Queen Alexandra, the wife of Edward VII, which was used in 1902 to crown her at their coronation. In 1911 it was set in the crown of Queen Mary, who wore it at the coronation of her husband George V. Later it was incorporated in the crown of Elizabeth, wife of George VI, for his coronation in 1937. Now known as the Queen Mother's Crown, it comprises 2,800 diamonds, among them a 17-carat (3.4 g) Turkish diamond given to Queen Victoria in 1856 by Abdülmecid I, Sultan of the Ottoman Empire, as a gesture of thanks for British support in the Crimean War. The Koh-i-noor is set in the cross at the front of the crown. When the Queen Mother died in 2002 it was placed on top her coffin for her lying-in-state and funeral. It is now secured in the Jewel House at the Tower of London along with the other crown jewels, and may be viewed by the curious citizen or overseas visitor for £24.80.

FIVE

MOST LOYAL SUBJECT

During his first years in England Duleep Singh occupied
various houses in London. They were rented for him by
Login, who continued to be responsible for his upbringing,
a task that brought him a knighthood. Between them
the Queen and the Logins introduced Duleep Singh to
an aristocratic social circle, where he became a popular
figure, as much because of his natural charm and sociable
temperament, as the curiosity he aroused by his unusual
appearance and the sympathy many people, taking a lead
from the Queen, felt for his circumstances.

Login kept Dalhousie informed about the Maharajah's
education. He wrote to say they had been reading about
the Sikhs together, in particular a book called *A History of
the Reigning Family of Lahore* published in 1847 and edited

by Major Carmichael Smith.[xc] 'I have thought it right that he should be aware that everything regarding his early history is known in England, and that the attention and kindness which have been shown him have been caused by a desire to encourage him to raise himself out of the mire of treachery, murder and debauchery, in which, but for God's grace, he would have been overwhelmed.'[xci]

A chapter in Carmichael Smith's book was devoted to Duleep Singh's birth and parentage, where he would have learnt that he had little claim to a 'dignified paternity', and that his mother's conduct as a young teenager had been 'loose and immodest'. Instead of being taught to take pride in the achievements of his father, the Lion of the Punjab, who had been the architect of the kingdom of the Sikhs and the only maharajah with whom the British had felt it necessary to enter into a treaty of friendship, he was being urged to feel shame. Not only had he been deprived of everything material that he might have inherited, but he was being given lessons in self-hatred, or at least self-contempt.

However, at this stage of his life Duleep Singh does not appear to have been greatly downhearted. His education in the school of life was being taken in hand by his great friend, the Prince of Wales, with whom he 'happily gambled and whored' his way round the capital.[xcii] In December 1856 Login and his wife added a more respectable dimension to his gentlemanly upbringing by taking him on a trip to France and Italy. (At the head of her chapter describing their holiday Lady Login added the imperishable words, 'Readers already satiated with descriptions of Italian travel are recommended to skip this chapter.'[xciii]) In Rome they dined with John Bright and his 'pretty' daughter. Lady Login recorded in her travel diary that they were a merry party: 'Mr Bright [was] very eloquent about the *wrongs* of India, to the Maharajah's infinite amusement!'[xciv]

On their return Login leased Castle Menzies in Perthshire, where Duleep Singh discovered the joys of grouse shooting and was persuaded to wear a kilt. He was able to revive his passion for hawking, a sport that had almost become extinct in Scotland, thus creating a rare link with his life at home.

An engraving of the Maharajah appeared in *The Drawing Room Portrait Gallery of Eminent Persons of 1859*, and was based on a photograph taken by John Mayall, now in the royal collection. It shows Duleep Singh in a state of transition: already beginning to put on weight, he still wears his turban for a formal portrait, as well pearls, jewels and ear drops, ornaments that were such a notable feature of Winterhalter's oil portrait, but the silks and robes have disappeared, and in their place he wears a frock coat and trousers, which though exotically braided and decorated are unmistakably a version of western dress.

While living in Castle Menzies, he was informed that his residence in Fatehgarh had been sacked and burnt down in 1857 during the Mutiny, and that his servants had been murdered. He had left valuable property in his *toshkhana* (treasury) in Fatehgarh to be guarded by his English steward, Sergeant A. Elliott. This man, together with his wife and children, his old tutor and other European residents were all murdered. The scale of his loss was estimated by Login, who made a claim on the Maharajah's behalf:

Value of property pillaged at Futtehghur.

	Rupees
Land and houses purchased by His Highness	93,014
Furniture and fittings of all descriptions, including table-furniture, plate, glass and crockery	74,403
Tent equipage made at Futtehghur	10,765
Farrash Khana property, consisting of Cashmere tents, carpets, Muslunda quilts, chogas, elephant jhools, &c	20,000
	198,182

These sums are difficult to compute into modern money, but using the rate of fifteen rupees to the pound, the grand total of the Maharajah's claim was in the order of £13,200. By way of compensation the British government offered him £3,000, which he refused to accept, 'considering the proposition an insult'. The words are those of Lady Login, who clearly felt he had indeed been insulted.[xcv]

Duleep Singh's exile was cushioned with luxury and privilege, but it was also fraught with confusion. Every aspect of his new identity was ambivalent: he was neither Indian nor British; he was a maharajah, addressed as Your

Highness, but had no power to rule and no kingdom to rule over; he enjoyed the life of a British aristocrat, but had no land or heritage on which to draw either his income or his status, for he was in effect a pensioner of the British state.

There was one area of his young life where these ambiguities were at their most intense. Who would make a suitable wife for Duleep Singh to marry? He mixed with members of the aristocracy, but would their hospitality and friendship extend as far as allowing him to marry one of their daughters? By the same token, did he wish to marry a British woman, or did he prefer the idea of a bride from India? And if so, who could fill the bill?

As it happened there was a suitable candidate in England: the Princess Victoria Gouramma of Coorg, a godchild of Queen Victoria, who had taken an interest in the girl after her father was deposed from his throne in 1834. She was of royal blood, she was pretty, she mixed in the same circles as the Maharajah, and she was a Christian convert. Though the Princess was only thirteen, Queen Victoria nursed romantic fantasies of bringing together her two royal Indian exiles, and she encouraged Duleep Singh to marry her when he first arrived in England. However, he resisted her match-making, telling Login that he intended to remain a bachelor.

During 1856 and 1857 the Maharajah received frequent invitations to Windsor and Osborne, and the Prince of Wales and Prince Alfred visited him in Ashburton Court, which he had temporarily rented. They shared a common interest in cricket and photography. In September 1858

Duleep Singh turned nineteen. He requested permission to manage his own affairs, which was granted, and his pension was increased to £15,000 per annum, a huge sum for a boy of his age to have at his disposal, but one that was far short of the four lakhs of rupees guaranteed by the Treaty of Lahore. He resided in a series of grand houses that were rented on his behalf, including Mulgrave Castle near Whitby, where he indulged his love of fishing and shooting game, and generally enjoyed what Lady Login coyly called his 'bachelor life'.[xcvi]

Although he appeared to lead the carefree and gilded existence that his income and position permitted, the authorities were concerned that he was nursing a desire to reconnect with his mother, a figure always regarded by the British in India as a pernicious influence and a potential source of insurrection. In 1860, the year he turned twenty-one, Duleep Singh's wish to see his mother intensified. Mindful of the loyalty shown by the Sikhs during the Mutiny, the British were obliged to tread carefully, for they did not want to incite hostility in the Punjab by refusing a son's natural request to see his mother. The government was reassured by the Resident in Nepal, who reported that 'The Rani had much changed, was blind and had lost much of her energy which formerly characterised her, taking apparently but little interest in what was going on'.[xcvii] In any case, Duleep Singh himself seemed to be as excited by the prospect of tiger-shooting as seeing his mother again. Permission for a visit to India was granted, on condition that he did not return to the Punjab. Jindan

Kaur was told that she could leave Nepal in order to travel to Calcutta, where her son would be staying.

The Maharajah landed in Calcutta in January 1861 and stayed in Spence's Hotel, generally considered the best in Calcutta. Whether to please his old guardian or not, Duleep Singh wrote to Login, saying, 'I must tell you that India is a beastly place!... The heat is something dreadful, and what will it be in another month. I hate the natives, they are such liars, flatterers, and extremely deceitful!' His meeting with his mother, the first in thirteen and a half years, must have been an emotional occasion for both of them. According to folklore, when the sightless Rani touched his face and then felt his head she was furious to discover that he had shorn his hair and betrayed his Sikh heritage.

Jindan Kaur declared that she never wanted to be parted from her son again. To avoid the heat Duleep Singh planned to take his mother to a house in the hills, but his trip had to be cut short. When the news spread that the Maharajah was present in the hotel, hundreds of Sikh soldiers, recently disembarked from a troop ship, gathered outside, chanting the Sikh victory cry. The Indian government wasted no time in arranging for mother and son to catch the next ship for England.

Though Jindan Kaur's health was broken, she still had the vitality to remind her son of the injustices done to him. In July 1861 Duleep Singh wrote to Login saying he would like to have a conversation about his 'private property in the Punjab and the Koh-i-noor diamond', and asked him to bring the Punjab Blue Book (the official government record.)[xcviii] This was regarded as a symptom of the Rani's malign effect on her son. Colonel Phipps, Keeper of the Privy Purse, articulated the anxieties felt in the palace: 'I fear very much,' he wrote to Login, 'that, as long as he remains under this influence [his mother's], he will retrograde in his moral and social character, instead of advancing to become an English gentleman, as I thought he was doing.'[xcix]

If his mother was standing in the way of his becoming an English gentleman, the obstacle was removed on 1 August 1863 when Jindan Kaur died. A distraught Duleep Singh telegrammed Login, who was ill himself, begging him to join him in London to help with arrangements for the disposal of his mother's remains. He wished to have her cremated in London, but was refused permission, cremation being illegal at that time. The body was placed temporarily in an unconsecrated vault in Kensal Green Cemetery until it could be taken to India and cremated according to Sikh practice. Many Indians gathered in the cemetery for the interment and Duleep Singh spoke a few words to the crowd in Hindustani. He compared the Christian religion with Hinduism and assured them that 'in the blood of Christ alone was their safety from condemnation in a future state.'[c]

By then Login had purchased Elveden Hall and its estate in Suffolk on Duleep Singh's behalf, and the Maharajah was keen that they should inspect the new purchase together, but before a meeting could be arranged Login himself died, on 18 October 1863, aged fifty-three. Duleep Singh's grief was 'most intense and unaffected.'[ci]

The funeral was held in Felixstowe and Duleep Singh was the chief mourner with Login's two sons. At the graveside many people heard him cry out, 'Oh, I have lost my *father!* – for he was, indeed, my father, and more than my father.' He told Lady Login, 'If *that* man is not in Heaven, then there is not one word of truth in the Bible!'[cii] (Emphases in the original.)

Duleep Singh proposed to build a mausoleum for Login and his family in Elveden, but Lady Login preferred to leave her husband's body in Felixstowe. Some years later Duleep Singh paid for a red granite and marble monument to stand on his grave, and composed the epitaph which reads:

> This monument is erected
> By his affectionate Friend and Ward,
> THE MAHARAJAH DULEEP SINGH
> In grateful remembrance of the
> Tender Care and Solicitude with which
> Sir John Login
> Watched over his early years,
> Training him up in the pure
> And simple faith of Our Lord and Saviour
> JESUS CHRIST

Any doubts concerning his commitment to Christianity must come to terms with both the many private letters in which he expresses his devotion to Christ, and public gestures such as this one and the words he spoke at the interment of his mother.

Duleep Singh had only just turned twenty-five when Login died. In the space of two months he lost both his mother and the man who was as close to a father as he had known. These two losses were added to the great tally of losses that he had already suffered during his short life. By ordinary standards he was a young man who appeared to have at his command a great many of life's enviable acquisitions – rank, money, property, connections, education – but these privileges had to be weighed against the singular deprivations inflicted on him from childhood onwards – kingdom, homeland, fortune, power, culture. And now he had lost what anybody of his age, rich or poor, could regard as natural entitlements – his mother and the man he regarded as his father. Although both Lady Login and the Queen continued to be greatly concerned for him throughout his troubled adulthood, no one ever replaced Login as the person whose advice he trusted and sought.

When assessing Duleep Singh's character, it should never be forgotten that he grew up without his own father – the father against whom he would always be measured, but whom history dictated that he could never emulate. Although he was lucky to have a father figure in the shape of Login, who was benign and affectionate, he was by no means a substitute father. Login had been his mentor, tutor and guardian, but he was neither a Sikh nor a king. Duleep Singh's behaviour – sometimes vainglorious, sometimes servile, and often self-destructive – can partly be attributed to living in the shadow of an esteemed, but absent father and to his lacking a satisfactory model of masculinity, either Sikh or British.

The immediate effect of these two deaths on Duleep Singh was that he made a decision that announced in unmistakable terms a new sense of independence.

He had been given permission to take his mother's remains back to India where he could arrange her cremation, and he set sail on 16 February 1864 with his mother's corpse on board. Breaking his journey in Cairo, he revisited the American Presbyterian Mission where he had been taken on his first journey to England in 1854. He wrote to the head of the mission, asking if he could recommend a girl in one his schools as a wife. 'Rank and position are of no consequence to me. What I want is a truly Christian girl who loves the Lord Jesus in sincerity and truth.'[iii] As luck would have it, there was an ideal candidate among the pupils: Bamba Müller, who was 'beautiful and unsophisticated, extremely winning in all her ways, and graceful, even queenly, in her movements.'[iv] Furthermore, she was a Christian Copt, who had recently spent several months 'under deep conviction of sin,'[v] but had finally 'found the Christian's joy in life.'[vi] As for rank and position, she could hardly have come from a humbler background, for she was the illegitimate daughter of a German businessman and 'an Abyssinian slave', a woman 'who had brought up her child in the simple Eastern style to which she was herself accustomed.'[vii] Duleep Singh brushed aside all objections, and declared that Bamba sounded perfect. (Her name means 'pink'.)

Leaving behind a 'very handsome' ring and bracelet for Bamba to keep, whether or not she accepted him, Duleep

Singh then departed for Bombay. The mission staff hastily prepared his bride-to-be for her new life. Among other things, they had to teach her a new way to eat, since she was accustomed to sitting on the floor and had no idea how to use a knife and fork. The fact that she was fifteen years old did not seem to trouble anyone involved in these nuptials – not her parents, not the missionaries, certainly not her ardent fiancé. (At the time the age of consent in England was twelve; it was raised to sixteen in 1885.)

On 7 June 1864 Duleep Singh and Bamba were married, first in a civil ceremony at the British consulate in Cairo and later in a Christian ceremony. Because she was still learning English, Bamba made her vows in Arabic. Before leaving Cairo the Maharajah presented the mission with £1,000 in Bamba's name as a thank-offering, and undertook to donate £500 per year during the remainder of their lives.

Despite being a Maharajah, Duleep Singh had been dictated to all his life – by his mother, by Dalhousie and the British and Indian authorities, by the Queen, by Login; he had never been allowed to make his own decisions concerning his affairs. On this occasion, however, he took the initiative without seeking anyone's advice or permission, and without informing the authorities in England of his intentions.

How to explain the impetuous and ruthless way in which he went about acquiring a wife? Indeed, how to explain his choice? Bamba herself, apart from having impeccable credentials as a devout Christian, played a very small part in his selection. What seems to have recommended her to him was her youth and innocence, and her humble circumstances; she was completely defenceless and therefore eminently trainable as a 'helpmeet' (his word for what he wanted in a wife).[cviii] At no point during the bizarre train of events in Cairo did he make any attempt to form even the sketchiest relationship with Bamba before making his proposal. It is hard not to conclude that Duleep Singh, weary of submitting to other people's bidding, had finally seized this chance to impose his will on someone who was entirely at his mercy. It was not a good basis for a marriage.

After their wedding the couple sailed to England, where Duleep Singh gave instructions for the reconstruction of Elveden Hall, before taking his bride back to Egypt on a honeymoon. Bamba made a favourable impression on Colonel Oliphant, the Maharajah's equerry, who reported to the Queen that 'In person she is small and delicately made, has a sweet smile, winning expression, a soft black eye... She is unable to speak English as yet ... but she is quite self-possessed and has a natural dignity of manner.'[cix] For his part, the Maharajah showed every sign of being besotted with his new wife. A year or so later the Queen invited the couple to stay at Windsor. By then Bamba appears to have acquired sufficient savoir faire to hold her own at court, a remarkable achievement. The Queen recorded the visit in her journal: 'the good Maharajah (in his Indian dress) & his lovely little wife, beautifully dressed in Indian stuffs, covered with splendid jewels

& pearls, like a Princess in a fairy tale, dined. He is so amiable & agreeable, but gets too fat.[tx]

Once Duleep Singh was married and had taken up residence in Elveden Hall, Lady Login saw less of him. She did comment that on one of her infrequent visits to the Hall, 'he was much occupied with religious meetings, in which he took a prominent part.'[txi] Despite their separation, she remained a staunch supporter of the Maharajah throughout his life, and was always sympathetic to his pleas of injustice against the government.

Duleep Singh and Bamba made Elveden Hall their home in 1865, and it was here that their first surviving child, a son, was born in the summer of the following year. Victor was to be the first of the six children, three boys and three girls, whom Bamba produced between 1866 and 1879, when her last son was born.[cxii]

In Duleep Singh's hands, Elveden Hall became a luxurious mansion, a fitting palace for a maharajah to inhabit and entertain members of the British royal family and the aristocracy. He turned Elveden into one of England's great shooting estates, becoming a famous shot himself. By 1873 the estate had been extended to 14,615 acres, and when the Prince of Wales paid his third visit three years later the Maharajah's gamekeepers were able to provide the royal shooting party with a bag of close to 6,000 birds, nearly 4,500 of them pheasants.[cxiii]

By all accounts Duleep Singh was a benign landlord and a conscientious steward of his estate, but as the years went by he began to neglect Elveden and his family in favour of more metropolitan pleasures. He grew very stout and became 'a notorious playboy'.[cxiv] On his occasional visits to Paris he had affairs with several well-known courtesans, though in London his taste was more for actresses, showgirls and chambermaids, among them a certain Ada Wetherill who worked at Cox's Hotel. He loved the Alhambra Theatre, a disreputable haunt for men hoping to make sexual liaisons with dancers and showgirls, where he could be seen 'graciously accepting the homage of the houris in the green room, and distributing 9 carat gimcracks with oriental lavishness.[txv] Waving a piece of jewellery, he would ask, 'What nice little girl is going to have this?'[txvi] Nor did he confine his infidelities to London. Several housemaids and other female servants at Elveden lost their positions by becoming pregnant, and their illegitimate sons were known locally as the 'young princes'. In some cases he paid for their education and upbringing, a minor expense compared with the presents, annuities and properties he bestowed on the objects of his infatuations in London. Polly Ash, for example, an Alhambra dancer with whom be became obsessed, was rewarded with a flat in Covent Garden and £2,000 a year for life.[cxvii]

Duleep Singh lived beyond his means all his life, and at the same time he was perpetually aggrieved, with some justification, by the government's repeated failure to honour the financial terms of the 1849 Treaty of

Lahore. For example, when he was twenty-one years old, the government decided after much prevarication that he should receive a pension of £25,000, an enormous sum, but still below the minimum that had been guaranteed him in the Treaty. He asked that it should be raised to £35,000, but his request was deemed 'unreasonable'. As the Secretary to the India Board pointed out, 'With £25,000 he is far above the average of peers and *noblemen* in this country and indeed I believe that the overall income of the House of Lords is under £10,000.'[lxxviii] This may well have been true, but Duleep Singh's point that he had been short-changed under the Treaty was still valid, and it rankled with him all his life.

Despite continually complaining about the injustice of his restricted budget, Duleep Singh did little to curb his expenses, which were compounded by his gambling losses and a drop in agricultural prices. In 1878 Coutts Bank demanded at least part-repayment of a £40,000 loan, and by the next year his financial position became so dire that for once the government listened to his appeals for aid. It was agreed that he should be given an interest-free loan of £57,000 to pay his debts, on condition that the Elveden estate was sold on his death to recover the loan and the money the government had originally advanced as a mortgage. He was forced to accept these terms, but he claimed to be heart-broken on behalf of his eldest son, who would not inherit his old home. He confided his feelings to the Queen: 'No one knows but myself, my Sovereign, the agony that I suffered when I was turned out of my house and exiled from the land of my birth and I shudder to think of the sufferings that my poor boy may undergo.[lxix]

In 1879 Bamba gave birth to her sixth and last child, a son, whom the Maharajah named Albert Edward, in yet another attempt to keep in the Queen's good graces. However, by now it was obvious to Bamba that her husband was neither faithful nor even discreet. In 1881 Duleep Singh virtually abandoned his family and Elveden by renting a house in Holland Park in London, which allowed him to be close to Polly Ash and his other mistresses. The marriage was over in all but name.

Already embittered by his treatment at the hands of the Indian government, Duleep Singh now went on the offensive and wrote a long letter to *The Times* detailing the many wrongs done to him by the British from childhood onwards, among them the failure to compensate him for the loss of earnings from his private properties and income. Meanwhile, he was reduced to begging once again for money from the government, but he received a cold refusal from the Under-Secretary of State for India. The Queen was asked to intercede on his behalf, but the India Office remained obdurate. His friends were warning that the Maharajah was threatening to sell what remained of his jewels and treasure in order to maintain Elveden. There were even rumours that he was proposing to quit England altogether and return to India.

In 1883 he reappeared in Elveden and, to the horror of his family, stripped the place of his most valuable possessions and put them up for auction. The catalogue for the three-day sale announced the sale of 25,000 ounces of chased plate, including twenty-four breakfast services made of silver and gilt plate, rare Indian carpets, cashmere shawls, and a 'casket of jewels'. The announcement also contained the explanation that the sale was 'preparatory to [the Maharajah's] leaving England for India'.[cxx]

There was still sympathy for the Maharajah's situation, and the sale prompted questions in the House of Commons about his compensation under the Treaty of Lahore. Duleep Singh himself appealed directly to the Queen, stating his case yet again, this time in his own handwriting, 'as a last resort before quitting the country'.[cxxi] The Queen wrote a mollifying reply, saying that she doubted it was in his interests to visit India, but she had no desire to restrict his movements if he thought that 'a voyage to the East would be conducive to your amusement, health and comfort'.[cxxii]

For some time Duleep Singh had been engaged in research, working in the British Library on the Blue Books for India during the period of the Punjab's annexation. In July 1884 he printed his book, *Maharajah Duleep Singh and the Government*, referred to above, in which he accused the Indian government of maltreating him. He had a point, but by then no one was listening.

As he distributed his book Duleep Singh wrote to Sir Henry Ponsonby, the Queen's private secretary, enclosing a paper knife as a gift for the Queen. The handle was made of gold and red coral, and it was inscribed with the motto 'VR1 *fidelitus*'. In his most respectful tone, he begged Ponsonby to lay his gift 'at the feet of [his] Sovereign', saying that he had ordered the handle specially for her when he was last in Naples on a visit with his sons. Then, in mid-paragraph, his tone abruptly changed: 'as I have been a most loyal subject to the Crown for the last 35 years I shall not therefore now turn traitor although I may re-embrace the faith of my ancestors...' He informed Ponsonby that before departing for India he intended to lay before Her Majesty his reasons for doing so. Referring to Russian hostilities on the North West Frontier, he commented ominously that 'There is a terrible storm gathering in India. I know that the advent of Russia [in India] is hailed with intense joy both by the people and the Princes of India in their secret hearts whatever they may outwardly say and they are all prepared to rebel as soon as that Power advances a little nearer.'[txxiii] He was reaching the end of his tether.

By now the Maharajah was in touch with his cousin, Sardar Thakur Singh Sandhawalia, whom he commissioned to put together a report on the state and extent of his private property in the Punjab. In September 1884 Thakur Singh left Amritsar with several members of his family, including a Sikh priest, to visit the Maharajah in London and Elveden. As Peter Bance described it, 'the Sikh entourage moved down to the Suffolk estate, where mischievous, turbaned Sikhs could be seen moving round the Hall and plotting the fall of British rule in the Punjab.'[txxiv]

A year later Duleep Singh informed the government that he intended to leave England for India, where he would be able to provide a home for his family that would not be sold on his death. He also intended to be reinitiated into the Sikh faith. In March 1886 the Indian government made a final offer of £50,000, on condition that he abandoned his claim to any property in India and gave an undertaking never to return to India. It was too late. The Maharajah rejected this 'paltry sum'[txxv] and on 31 March he boarded SS *Verona* with all his family to embark on the first leg of their voyage to Bombay. He left behind instructions for the entire contents of Elveden Hall and its farm to be auctioned.

His plans for their future life in India were not clear. Whatever they were, they were thwarted in Aden, where the Maharajah, now dressed in Sikh regalia, was presented with a warrant for his arrest. The government had changed its mind. He was offered the chance to return to England providing he would pledge not to renew his attempt to travel to India. He refused, but decided to send his family back. While still detained at Aden he asked permission, which was granted, to undergo a ceremony of reinitiation into Sikhism. For the occasion he also requested a suitably regal retinue, consisting of a Sikh granthi (reader of the scriptures), an attendant with a copy of the Granth, Hindu cooks, Hindu water-carriers, valets and attendants, including a washerman, tailor, sweeper and musketeer. In the event, he had to make do with the few Sikhs who happened to be in Aden on the day. On 25 May 1886 the Resident, General Hogg, was able to send a cable to the Governor-General in Shimla: 'After much delay, the

Maharajah was remade a Sikh this morning. I was not present nor did I in any way countenance the same…'[cxxvi]

Suffering badly from the heat, the new convert fell ill, and Hogg feared that both his health and his sanity were being affected. The Maharajah alarmed the authorities in India and London by suggesting that he should be given a public trial, an appalling prospect with the Queen's jubilee approaching. In the same breath he declared that he was renouncing his stipend under the Lahore Treaty, 'thus laying aside that iniquitous document.'[cxxvii]

It was a great relief to all concerned when on 3 June the Maharajah boarded a French mail-steamer bound for Marseille.

There is no need to dwell on the remainder of the Maharajah's biography, which makes painful reading.

He took up residence in Paris, where he was joined by the seventeen-year-old Ada Wetherill, one of the chambermaids he had met at Cox's Hotel in London.[cxxviii] Back in London, Bamba and the children made their home in the old house in Holland Park. His eldest son, Victor, wrote to his father, asking for money, but his request was rejected. 'Look upon me as dead,' Duleep Singh instructed him.[cxxix]

Though increasingly ill and always desperate for money, the Maharajah took encouragement from his Punjabi advisors and entangled himself in a doomed plot to regain his throne. 'With the help of God of my fathers,' he wrote in a letter, 'I will for once at least overthrow the tyrannical, immoral and unscrupulous administration of India.'[xxxx] If the Tsar of Russia would only send 10,000 men to the North West Frontier, Punjabis now in the British army, his former subjects, would immediately come over to his side and then the whole of the Punjab would follow. In order to effect this hare-brained scheme he fell into the company of various Russian and Fenian conspirators, one of them a British double-agent, who reported back to London his every move – his visitors, his letters, his conversations.

Duleep Singh wrote to Alexander III, representing himself as 'an unfortunate Indian Prince, one of the monuments of British injustice'. He implored the Tsar to find a safe asylum in Russia for 'one of your most loyal subjects.'[cxxxi] The letter was copied by the double-agent and sent to London. Duleep Singh was persuaded that he should ask for the Tsar's help in person. Armed with a passport that identified him as Patrick Casey, which in fact belonged to a Fenian revolutionary, he and Ada took the train to Berlin on 21 March 1887. Their disguise was not improved by the fact that they were accompanied by a Sikh servant, two spaniels and so many trunks, hatboxes and pieces of luggage that many of them had to be abandoned. At Berlin the Maharajah's purse, which contained the funds for his trip and his false passport, was stolen. The German police took a statement from this improbable Irishman, and then allowed him to resume his journey.

The Maharajah and Ada languished in Moscow while he waited with increasing frustration for his summons to St Petersburg for an audience with the Tsar. On 10 May 1887 he wrote a long memorandum to Alexander from his hotel, laying out a battle plan for their mutual advantage. He asked nothing for himself except the opportunity 'to deliver some 250,000,000 of [his] countrymen from the cruel yoke of British Rule'. He informed the Tsar that on behalf of the princes of India he was authorised to say that, when freed and managing their own affairs, they would join together to pay an annual tribute into the Russian treasury of £3,000,000. 'I guarantee an easy conquest of India,' he wrote, and by way of reassurance he quoted a Sikh prophecy which predicted that 'a man bearing my name would after becoming deposed [dispossessed] of all he had inherited and after residing alone in a foreign country for a long time, return and with the aid of a European power free the Sikhs from the cruel bondage that they would be then suffering under for their sins.' Finally, he told the Tsar that, having made his appeal on behalf of his countryman, he considered his duty done. 'If graciously permitted by the Emperor to enjoy both liberty and safety in his Majesty's dominions, I shall occupy myself in sport leaving the Almighty to bring about the deliverance of my unfortunate people in His own good time.'[lxxxii]

At the end of May Duleep Singh was notified that his letter had been read with much interest in St Petersburg, and that he was free to reside and travel everywhere within Russia. He continued to wait in Moscow for his invitation to meet the Tsar. But then, in quick succession, he received two blows, which brought to an end his hopes for reclaiming his Punjabi throne. In August his Russian representative at the imperial court died, leaving him helpless and without influence. Later that month he heard that his cousin and so-called 'prime minister in exile', Thakur Singh Sandhwalia, had died in Pondicherry under mysterious circumstances.

Duleep Singh was still in Moscow when the news reached him that the Maharani Bamba had died, aged thirty-nine, on 18 September 1887. Broken by Duleep Singh's behaviour, she had become a virtual alcoholic. She was buried in the churchyard at Elveden, but her husband did not attend the funeral. The Prince of Wales sent him a letter, but Duleep Singh angrily rejected his condolences: '...while your illustrious mother proclaims herself the Sovereign of a Throne and of an Empire which have been acquired by fraud and of which Y.R.H. also hopes one day to become the Emperor, these empty conventional words addressed to me amount to an insult.[cxxxiii]

On 26 December 1887 Ada gave birth to a daughter in Moscow. The following day her father sent a telegram to his contact in Paris, saying, 'Failure. I leave for Paris.'[cxxxiv] He was reported to be in great financial difficulty, spending days and nights on his own, weeping repentantly. In fact, he and Ada did not return to Paris immediately. The Russian authorities had lost patience with him and he was instructed to leave Moscow and confine himself discreetly in Kiev in the Ukraine. It was clear that the longed-for interview with the Tsar was never going to take place. If there had ever been a moment when the invasion of India had seemed feasible to the Russians, with or without the invaluable assistance of the Maharajah, it had passed. The Great Game had left him off the board, and he was obliged to swallow yet another humiliation.

He had been ruinously advised by his Sikh collaborators and Fenian co-conspirators, he had been duped by the British government, and he had succumbed to vainglorious fantasies of restoration, while getting completely out of his depth in international politics. Throughout his adult life he felt he had been cheated and betrayed by those in charge of his destiny, and when an opportunity to reverse the ignominious pattern of his life was whispered in his ear, he naively snatched at it. Who can blame him for believing that his birthright was still owing to him, and still worth reclaiming? The inscription on the statue in Thetford states that he intended to return to his 'beloved' Punjab to reclaim his throne. Perhaps it would be truer to say that by 1886 he had finally found it impossible to live with his identity as an exile, and that what he was hoping to reclaim, as much as his kingdom, title and wealth, was his identity as a Sikh.

Disillusioned and still more deeply impoverished, Duleep Singh finally returned to Paris with Ada on 3 November 1888. Ada was soon pregnant again, and on 21 May of the following year she and the Maharajah were married in a civil ceremony in the mayor's office of the eighth *arrondissement*, having previously undergone a wedding according to Sikh rites. Ada took the title Maharani, but it was never officially recognised.

Duleep Singh was forced to sell the last of his jewels; he began to drink heavily and suffered from diabetes. Despite her new title, which she used for the rest of her life, Ada was already bored with her sick and aged husband by the spring of 1890, and she separated herself informally from the Maharajah, who could only afford to live in cheap rooms on the fifth floor of a lodging house. On 13 July 1890 he had a stroke that paralysed his left side. He was given permission to make a visit to England for a month, and his elder sons organised a trip to Folkestone where all his children were gathered together for the last and only time.

Duleep Singh was now anxious to obtain the Queen's forgiveness, and he asked his son Victor to write to her requesting a pardon. A meeting was arranged in March 1891 'with the poor misguided Maharajah' when the Queen was on holiday in Grasse in the south of France. Accompanied by his second son Frederick, he attended on her at the Grand Hotel on 30 March and she recorded a detailed account of the occasion in both her journal and in a letter to her daughter Vicky. He was unable to kneel because his left arm and leg were still disabled. She invited him to sit down, whereupon 'almost directly he burst into a most terrible and violent fit of crying… I stroked & held his hand, & he became calm and said: "Pray excuse & forgive my faults" & I answered "They are forgotten and forgiven." He said: "I am a poor broken down man" … he seemed glad with the interview – but it was vy. sad –; still I am so glad that we met again & I cld. say I forgave him.'[txxxv]

This pathetic incident demonstrates yet again the importance of the Queen in the Maharajah's life, and for that matter his importance in hers. Despite the circumstances, she was still under the spell of his looks and charm: 'He is quite bald & vy. grey but has the same pleasant manner as ever.'[lxxxvi] She was one of the few stable figures remaining to him, and he never blamed her for the many outrages done to him in her name.

In April 1893, the Maharajah, very ill himself, was taken once again to England, this time to see his youngest son, Edward, who was dying of tuberculosis in Hastings. He kissed his son's hand and gave him a piece of paper on which he had written, 'The Lord is my Shepherd'. The boy died a week later and was buried beside his mother in Elveden; his father, now back in Paris, was too weak to attend the funeral.

In October 1893, while Ada and his son Frederick were in London, looking for a small house where he might live, Duleep Singh was alone in the Hotel de la Tremoille, Paris, though his little daughters by Ada called on him regularly with their nanny. On Saturday, 21 October, he summoned them three times, and on the last occasion gave them each a silver hawk's bell, which he had treasured since his boyhood. That night he had what was described as an apoplectic fit, and he was found dead the next day. He was fifty-five.

In his will Duleep Singh had expressed a wish to be buried wherever he died, but his family and the authorities were united in wanting his body returned to England so he could be buried in Elveden. The plate on his coffin lid read, 'Duleep Singh, Maharajah of Lahore, GCSI.[1] Born 4th September 1838. Died 22 October 1893.'

---

[1] Knight Grand Commander of the Star of India

PART TWO

Six
KHALISTAN

A balance sheet of colonialism that does not have an entry on the colony's side under 'humiliation', showing a substantial figure, is a false document. Whatever gains colonising powers may bring and impose on their colonies, the colonised must always bear a heavy, sometimes catastrophic, loss in terms of self-respect.

Duleep Singh's life was a chronicle of humiliation, which he mostly bore with dignity. Sometimes he brought embarrassment on himself, sometimes he made a defiant gesture, sometimes he displayed admirable stoicism, but the pattern was relentless. Once deposed, he had no choice but to embrace subordination, an insupportable destiny. Throughout his life Duleep Singh struggled in vain to find a satisfactory identity – as a king without a kingdom, as a Sikh without a country, as an exile without a homeland. In the course of this struggle he made some choices that were dishonourable and some that were misguided, but it is hard to see how the outcome would have been improved if he had behaved differently. As the 1849 Treaty of Lahore made pitilessly clear, the British authorities wanted only one thing from him: obedience; otherwise, they had no interest in him, and no use for him. Queen Victoria nursed more creative ambitions on his behalf, hoping to turn him into a figure of contented (and decorative) submission by encouraging him to be an honorary British aristocrat. Insofar as he ever won the respect of his British hosts, it was the result of his prowess as a sportsman and his generosity as a host to other sportsmen at Elveden. But, much as he enjoyed shooting game, bags of pheasants were no substitute for a lost kingdom.

Despite his birth in Lahore and his death in Paris, Duleep Singh became essentially a British person, and therefore a figure with whom in later years the Sikh diaspora in Britain could rewardingly identify. As the pioneer Sikh immigrant to this country, Duleep Singh was the first to suffer what Sikh immigrants were to suffer in their time; his humiliations prefigured theirs, and projected onto them a heroic quality. Thanks to him, their suffering had a princely precedent. By the same token, Duleep Singh symbolised the possibility of a modern recovery of Sikh pride. He had been a sacrificial victim, who stood for the loss suffered by all Sikhs; but he had also been a king, whose title could never be annulled, the son of a father whom the British had been obliged to fear and respect. Thus, he was a contradictory symbol: both scapegoat and redeemer.

The complex nature of his significance for British Sikhs helps to explain the symbolic and aesthetic choices made by those who commissioned his statue in Thetford.

The Sikhs have never completely recovered from the surrender of 1849 and the consequent loss of their independent kingdom. However, the Treaty of Lahore, though politically crushing, did not displace them from the Punjab or destroy them economically. They had always been an agricultural community, and they thrived as they continued to inhabit the most fertile part of the sub-continent. Nor did they lose their cultural identity, which was a tribute to the strength of their religion. The British were able to exploit and reinforce another feature of their identity, the warrior tradition, by recruiting them into the army. During the Mutiny of 1857-58 Sikh soldiers had remained loyal to the Indian government, (more out of aversion to the prospect of a return to Hindu or Muslim rule, than love of the imperial regime) and thereafter the Sikhs enjoyed a measure of favoured status. British regulations ordered that Sikh soldiers should be allowed to keep their beards and long hair, privileges that were also enjoyed by Sikh civil servants.

When the First World War began, the British army was forced to recruit as many soldiers as it could from its empire. The Sikhs volunteered in large numbers, and by the end of the war there were 100,000 Sikhs in uniform, who represented about a fifth of the army then in action. Sikh battalions fought in Egypt, Palestine, Mesopotamia, Gallipoli and France. Of the twenty-two military crosses awarded for conspicuous gallantry to Indians, the Sikhs won fourteen.[cxxxvii]

This exemplary contribution did not bring the Sikhs the rewards they expected after the war, when Indian political leaders began to agitate for self-government. On the contrary, the authorities in the Punjab imposed severely repressive measures, which were followed by demonstrations, riots, and arrests. On 13 April 1919 troops of the British Indian Army under the command of Colonel Reginald Dyer fired machine guns into a crowd of unarmed civilians, most of them Sikhs, which had assembled to protest and celebrate a religious festival in the Jallianwala Bagh, a park in Amritsar. The shooting continued for ten minutes, at the end of which 379 people lay dead, according to the official count, though the Indian National Congress counted more than 1,000. Several thousands were injured.[cxxxviii] The Amritsar massacre has been described as 'by a long way the worst use of military force against a civilian crowd in British history'.[cxxxix] It probably hastened the end of British rule in India, and in the Punjab it provoked the foundation in 1920 of the Akali Dal, the political party that was to represent the Sikhs.

Any residual feelings of loyalty and hopes of special protection the Sikhs might have nursed in relation to the British were destroyed in 1947 when arrangements for Partition were revealed. A carving knife was placed on the Sikhs' jugular vein, to borrow Kushwant Singh's lurid phrase, as the British realised that by yielding to Muslim demands for an independent state they would have to bisect the Punjab.[cxl] When the blade was drawn, around forty per cent of the Sikh community found themselves on the Pakistan side of the new border. The migrations made necessary by the division of Punjab 'unleashed a holocaust unparalleled in history'.[cxli] Sikhs were far from innocent when it came to slaughtering Muslims and even Hindus, but they too suffered terrible losses. According to UNHCR estimates, 14 million people were displaced by the violence, as Muslims virtually disappeared from East Punjab, and Sikhs and Hindus likewise disappeared from West Punjab. The numbers of those who were killed will never be accurately known, but estimates range between several hundred thousand and two million.[cxlii] It will certainly never be discovered how many women on all sides were raped and abducted.

The Sikhs lost much else besides, notably several historic shrines and Lahore – Ranjit Singh's old capital, the Paris of the Punjab – which fell on the Pakistan side of the map when Sir Cyril Radcliffe drew his notorious 'line'. Partition not only deprived the Sikhs of half their traditional territory, but it forced them to submit to a new and unfriendly regime under the Indian National Congress. Instead of enjoying favoured status under the British, however illusory and fickle, they were now a beleaguered minority in what they feared would be a new nation dominated by Hindus. As it turned out, the huge exodus of Sikhs into East Punjab did at least have the effect of consolidating the community, the *panth*, in the new-born India.

Despite the appalling events of 1947, the Sikhs prospered during the years following Partition, and made agriculture in the new state of Punjab the most progressive and productive in India. However, there was a small but powerful section of the community represented by the Akali Dal party that disapproved of the decadent life-style, as it was seen by the party, which this prosperity encouraged in Punjab. The Akali Dal began to campaign on behalf of the Sikhs in Punjab for official recognition as a separate community, isolated from Hindus, with its own state inside the federation of India, to be known as Khalistan – 'Land of the Khalsa'.

After many years of bitter and quarrelsome talks, punctuated by occasional violence, Indira Gandhi finally agreed to the Punjab Reorganisation Act in 1966, whereby Punjab was divided into three new states on the basis of language: the Hindi-speaking states of Haryana and Himachal Pradesh, and a much diminished Punjabi-speaking state that retained the name Punjab. The new Punjab became the only state in India with a Sikh majority population (fifty-eight per cent in 2011).

The Sikhs remained at odds with the Indian government. In the wake of a disastrous result in the Punjab Assembly election of 1972, the Akali Dal appointed a committee to draw up a new declaration of the party's policies. The result was the Anandpur Sahib Resolution of 1973. Although essentially a religious document committing the party to 'the propagation of Sikhism, its ethical values and code of conduct to combat atheism', it also contained a series of secular resolutions.[cxliii] In political terms, the Resolution demanded an autonomous region within the federation of India where 'Sikh interests [were] constitutionally recognised as the fundamental State policy' on the basis of 'having all powers to and for itself',[cxliv] except for foreign relations and defence.

Mrs Gandhi dismissed the Resolution as a secessionist document, but it represented the party's most ambitious attempt to formulate a separate and protected identity for the Sikhs. Since Partition the Sikhs had feared political and cultural domination by the Hindu majority. One can sense both fear and rage in the language used in the third paragraph of the Resolution's preamble (a translation from the original Punjabi): 'Whereas, the brute majority in India, in 1950, imposed a constitutional arrangement in India which denied the Sikhs their political identity and cultural popularity, thus liquidating the Sikhs politically and exposing them to spiritual death and cultural decay leading inevitably to their submergence and dissolution into the saltish sea waters of incoherent Hinduism...'[cxlv]

Relations between the Sikhs and Mrs Gandhi were always difficult, especially during the period of direct rule under the Emergency of 1975-77, when the Sikhs felt they had been singled out for unjust treatment. However, in 1984 things came to a catastrophic climax. After a long period of indecision, Mrs Gandhi finally concluded that she had to take extreme measures against Jarnail Singh Bhindranwale, a fundamentalist Sikh leader, who had allied himself with the Khalistan cause and provoked conflict throughout the state by exploiting Sikh anxieties concerning Hindu hegemony. 'This [Sikh] crisis of identity was the sore from which Bhindranwale squeezed such hatred of Hindus. His fundamentalism was founded not on love or fear of God, but fear of Hinduism.[cxlvi]

Bhindranwale and his followers were implicated in several murders, including those of the owner of a chain of newspapers, famous for his opposition to Bhindranwale, and a senior policeman. Punjab was engulfed in violence, while Bhindranwale took refuge in the Golden Temple in Amritsar, where he and his followers began to assemble a formidable armoury, including machine guns and semi-automatic rifles. Bhindranwale himself carried a revolver and wore a cartridge belt. In October 1983 Sikh extremists stopped a bus travelling from Amritsar to Delhi, separated its Sikh and Hindu passengers, and shot the Hindus. Six people died and one was seriously injured. The next day Mrs Gandhi declared a state of emergency in Punjab, which was to last for more than ten years.

The government could not impose its authority without removing Bhindranwale from the Golden Temple complex, and on 1 June 1984 Mrs Gandhi ordered the army to begin Operation Blue Star. The army significantly underestimated the firepower Bhindranwale had collected in his stronghold, and it took tanks, heavy artillery, helicopters, commandos and frogmen to breach the heavily fortified temple and remove the Sikh militants during a siege that lasted until the army's final assault on 5 June. Bhindranwale was killed during the action. Terrible damage was done to the temple's structure and decoration. The temple library caught fire, and many priceless manuscripts were lost. According to figures issued by the army, 500 Sikh militants were killed in the siege, while 830 military personnel were killed and 2360 wounded.[cxlvii] Large numbers of civilians also died during the period of the siege, perhaps as many as 20,000.

Sikhs round the entire country were appalled and enraged. At eight cantonments (military stations) in different parts of India, over 4,000 Sikh soldiers deserted their regiments, killed their officers and tried to get to Amritsar.[cxlviii] Sikh opinion was further angered when the government attempted to place the whole responsibility for the temple attack on the Akali Dal, accusing the party of provoking and then failing to control Bhindranwale's extremism. The government published grossly inaccurate figures about the number of dead, stating, for example, that 554 'civilian-terrorists' were killed and 121 injured, whereas the figure seems likely to have been anything between 1,500 and 5,000, most of them innocent pilgrims, women and children. Nor did government figures acknowledge that many victims captured after the siege appeared to have been killed in cold blood.

In the months that followed the police applied brutal methods when suppressing alleged Sikh extremism throughout Punjab, which in turn provoked murderous reprisals. Village after village was surrounded, the houses of Sikhs were searched for arms, young men were taken for questioning, beaten up and tortured. So far from stamping out separatism, these actions turned Bhindranwale into a martyr, and incited many young men to resort to violence. Some escaped to Pakistan, then returned with weapons made easily purchasable with money sent by sympathisers in Britain, Canada and the United Sates.

On 31 October 1984 Indira Gandhi was assassinated outside her house by her two Sikh bodyguards. The news of her death triggered an outburst of murderous hostility against Sikhs in Delhi and elsewhere, which appeared to have been stoked rather than repressed by the administration, and it engulfed most of northern India. Kushwant Singh wrote: 'What followed Mrs Gandhi's assassination tells a sordid tale of administrative and political complicity in a massacre of innocents of dimensions not seen in India since it became an independent state.[txlix]

The ferocity of the slaughter was reminiscent of the homicidal frenzy that marked the days of Partition. After the assassination, senior politicians and police officers orchestrated pogroms of Sikhs in various cities

Maharajah Duleep Singh, Charles Stewart Hardinge, 1847 (Wikimedia Commons)

Portrait of Maharani Jind Kaur, George Richmond, 1862 (Wikimedia Commons)

Maharajah Ranjit Singh with some of his wives (Wikimedia Commons)

Maharajah Duleep Singh entering his palace in Lahore, Charles Stewart Hardinge, 1847: Duleep Singh returns to Lahore escorted by British troops at the end of the First Anglo-Sikh War (1845-46) (Wikimedia Commons)

Replica of the Koh-i-noor diamond on display in Amritsar (shankar s/Wikimedia Commons)

Lithograph of Duleep Singh as a young man

Maharani Bamba Singh

Duleep Singh, 1877 (Royal Collection Trust / © Her Majesty Queen Elizabeth II 2018)

Exterior Elveden Hall (Suffolk Record Office)

Interior Elveden Hall (Suffolk Record Office)

Shooting party outside Elveden Hall: Duleep Singh is seated in the front row between two of his children in bowler hats (Suffolk Record Office)

Statue of Maharajah Duleep Singh, Denise Dutton, 1999 (Fraser Harrison)

Detail of statue (Fraser Harrison)

Side view and inscription (Fraser Harrison)

Three legged bridge, Thetford. The leg on the right leads to Butten Island. (© Lucy Kayne)

Graves of Maharajah Duleep Singh, Maharani Bamba Singh and Prince Edward, St Andrew and St Patrick Church, Elveden (Fraser Harrison)

Members of the Gurdwara Baba Budha Sahib Ji Sikh temple in Peterborough outside the Ancient House Museum of Thetford Life (© Archant CM Ltd –Norfolk)

Portrait of Maharajah Duleep Singh, Franz Xaver Winterhalter, 1854
(Royal Collection Trust © Her Majesty Queen Elizabeth II 2018)

Casualty of War: A Portrait of Maharajah Duleep Singh, The Singh Twins, 2013
(National Museums of Scotland commission, copyright The Singh Twins
www.singhtwins.co.uk)

across India, killing at least 2,733 Sikhs in Delhi alone. Gangs of assailants burned Sikhs alive, raped women, and destroyed their gurdwaras, shops, factories and homes. Trains and buses were halted and Sikh passengers dragged out to be killed. The violence continued unabated for four days. Official Indian government reports stated that about 2,800 people, mostly Sikhs, were killed across India, but independent sources estimated the number of deaths at about 8,000.[cl] Witnesses reported that the police and army had not intervened, and in some case had even been complicit in the massacres, which were designed 'to teach the Sikhs a lesson'. None of the senior politicians or police officers identified by victims and eyewitnesses as organisers or perpetrators of the massacres was held criminally responsible.[cli] Rajiv Gandhi, Mrs Gandhi's son who became prime minister after her death, came close to condoning the violence by saying, 'When a mighty banyan tree falls, the earth beneath is bound to shake.'

These terrible events left the Sikhs feeling more beleaguered than ever, aliens in their own country. At the next election in December 1984 the Congress Party encouraged the Hindu majority to see Sikhs as traitors.

For the next decade Punjab continued to be the scene of mayhem and human rights abuse on an atrocious scale. Indian security forces arbitrarily detained, tortured, executed, and 'disappeared' tens of thousands of Sikhs in counter-insurgency operations.[clii] The security forces persecuted their victims through extortion and by destroying their crops, livestock, and buildings. They obstructed justice by intimidating witnesses and lawyers, detaining and torturing family members, and failing to comply with court orders to release detainees. In the 1994 report *Dead Silence: Legacy of Abuses in Punjab*, Human Rights Watch/Asia described the government counter-insurgency operations as 'the most extreme example of a policy in which the end appeared to justify any and all means, including torture and murder.[cliii]

For their part, Sikh militant organisations fought back, aiming their violence at civilians, state security forces, and Sikh political leaders thought to be negotiating with the government. It was estimated that 4,733 separatists were active in the state, fighting to force a fundamentalist version of Sikhism on villages. Reporting in 1999, Amnesty International stated that 'In recent years, members of these armed secessionist groups have killed hundreds of policemen, officials and politicians, members of rival Sikh groups as well as numerous Hindu and Sikh civilians, sometimes after keeping them hostage. Moreover, they have killed journalists and editors for what they had written or because they refused to write in the manner or language dictated by Sikh groups. They have also shot several members of the judiciary... They have threatened witnesses and potential witnesses to serious crimes committed for political purposes in apparent attempts to intimidate them and frustrate the judicial process... Armed Sikh groups have also reportedly tortured members of the police and security forces.[cliv]

Between 1984 and 1993 almost 30,000 people were killed in Punjab as a result of militant violence and counter-insurgency operations conducted by security forces. By the summer of 1991 such support as there had been for the extremists was draining away. The peasants had suffered extortion, murder and rape for too long, and the separatists no longer seemed to be inspired by religious or political conviction. The government ordered the army to put an end to violence in the state, and by the end of 1993 a semblance of law and order had been restored, which was reinforced by a vigorous police campaign. It took nearly 250,000 military and para-military personnel to eliminate most of the militant groups operating in Punjab.[clv]

Both Partition and the horrific events of 1984 prompted large waves of Sikh emigration to Britain and elsewhere, but it is difficult to know the exact size of the British diaspora before 2001. The census of that year was the first to include a category for religious identification, and it revealed that there were 336,179 British people then describing their religion as Sikhism, of whom the great majority lived in England.

For these British Sikhs the situation in Punjab, and India at large, was always a matter of urgent concern. Prior to 1984 the British gurdwaras showed a degree of sympathy for the idea of Khalistan embodied in the Anandpur Sahib Resolution and raised funds for the cause. But Operation Blue Star changed everything. A rally held in Hyde Park attracted at least 25,000 Sikhs (unofficial estimates suggested 50-60,000), who then marched on the Indian High Commission, shouting 'Khalistan Zindabad!' (Long Live Khalistan!). The massacres following the assassination of Mrs Gandhi provoked even more outrage in Britain, and the violence in Punjab was reflected by turbulence and bitter dispute among British Sikh communities and political organisations. Some groups and parties campaigned for Khalistan, while others worked to publicise the human rights abuses taking place in Punjab. Indo-British relations were badly strained, as the Indian government accused the British of failing to control the Sikh community's support for what was described as terrorism.

According to Kushwant Singh, 'almost every terrorist organization in the Punjab had its counterpart in Britain, Canada and the United States, and collections were regularly made in gurdwaras for remittance to the parent bodies in India.'[clvi] Several acts of violence occurred outside India in the immediate aftermath of the killing of Sikhs in 1984. The most serious took place in June 1985 when an Air India plane crashed off the coast of Ireland as a result of a bomb and 329 passengers and crew were killed. At the same time a bomb exploded in Tokyo's Narita airport, and two porters who were handling Air India baggage were killed. It turned out that the destruction of the plane had been planned by members of a group in Amritsar to avenge Operation Blue Star on its first anniversary.[clvii]

The majority of British Sikhs repudiated these events and were horrified by them, but it was inevitable that Sikhism became associated in the public mind with extremism, to the great discomfort and embarrassment of the Sikh community. For a time those who favoured Khalistan were a dominant influence in the gurdwaras, the community's major resource, but as the violence persisted in Punjab their influence began to wane.[clviii] Loyalties began to shift as more and more Sikhs made successful careers in business and the professions, while also playing a significant part in British politics, both local and national. The proportion of British-born Sikhs was steadily increasing (they now form the majority) and they tended to identify more closely with Britain and British social values, which further reduced the sway of the neo-Khalistanis in the gurdwaras.

The Khalistan movement led to an uncomfortable period in Anglo-Sikh relations, but when British Sikh leaders lobbied in favour of the royal visit to Punjab in 1997 it was clear that support for the idea of Khalistan had faded. In a show of loyalty, a delegation flew to Amritsar to welcome the Queen 'on behalf of British Sikhs'.

SEVEN

'TURBANED INVASION'

The decade following the Operation Blue Star in 1984 saw some of the darkest days in the history of the Punjab, and it is worth remembering that they provided the context in which Sikh communities in both India and Britain laid their plans to commemorate the centenary of Duleep Singh's death, due to occur in 1993.

To that end the Maharaja Dalip (*sic*) Singh Memorial Trust was created in New Delhi. On 25 March 1991 the president of the Trust wrote a letter to the prime minister of the UK, at that time John Major, outlining its ambitions for honouring the memory of the Maharajah in the land of his exile. Under the subject heading '[A] PROPOSAL TO INSTITUTE A BEFITTING MEMORIAL FOR MAHARAJA DALIP SINGH SON OF MAHARAJA

RANJIT SINGH', the Trust first provided the Prime Minister with a potted history of Duleep Singh's brief reign, dethronement by the British and exile. Then came the nub of its request. In order to perpetuate the memory of Duleep Singh, the Trust desired that 'a suitable befitting Memorial may be raised in a dignified manner in London with the kind cooperation and help of the British Government at the very place where the Maharaja and his wife were buried. That a particular plot of land may be given on lease to the Trust so that we can plan to establish a befitting Memorial.' By giving favourable consideration to this proposal the Prime Minister would 'assuage the feelings of millions of Sikhs living in India and abroad', who feared that the memory of their last maharajah was gradually being obliterated.[clix]

This heartfelt request was put in the hands of the Delhi Sikh Gurdwara Management Committee in New Delhi and forwarded to London with a covering letter pleading for 'a Sikh museum at the place, where the last Maharaja (King) of the Sikhs was buried in London just outside his Palace at Elvdean (*sic*) 80 miles from London.[clx]

A laconic comment at the top of the second letter, presumably written by a civil servant, reads, 'want Museum for Sikh Maharaja.' In August 1991 the London Museum Officer replied on behalf of the Prime Minister. She diplomatically informed the Trust that while its desire for a memorial was appreciated, the way forward was not 'necessarily clear', since Elveden Hall was privately owned by Lord Iveagh. She added that the hall itself was empty and the public were only allowed into the grounds. However, she noted that the museum in Thetford had connections with the Maharajah's son, and recommended that the Trust contact Oliver Bone, curator of the Ancient House Museum, 'who would be happy to discuss proposals for a memorial with you'.[clxi] The letter was copied to Oliver Bone, who had already been consulted.

From the archive kept at the Ancient House Museum in Thetford we learn that contact was established between Bone and the Trust, which in March 1992 appointed him Honorary Chairman of its executive council. The letter from the President, Kulmohan Singh, confirming his appointment ended on a slightly threatening note. 'I have great hope,' the President wrote, 'that you will not disappoint my Council'.[clxii]

In May 1992 Kulmohan Singh paid a visit to Thetford. Around that time the Trust drew up a 'History and Proposal' describing the memorial it had in mind. The document laid out another brief account of Duleep Singh's life, mentioning his purchase of Elveden Hall and its land in 1863. (The Guinness family would have been surprised to read that the Maharajah's estate 'was managed by the Earl of Iveagh, appointed by him'.) It concluded by saying that after the Maharajah's death in Paris in 1893 his body was brought to England and 'cremated in the Church adjoining the Elveden Hall where his British wife Madam Bamba was earlier cremated'. This was, of course, not the case. As we have seen, the Maharajah was buried intact according to the rites of the Anglican Church, alongside his wife and youngest son. The proposal document acknowledged that Elveden Hall was in private hands, but claimed that the adjoining church, where 'the great hero of Sikh history' was buried, was not private property. Again, this was not the case. Although the church and its graveyard were one of the few bits of land that were not possessed by the owners of the Hall, they were nevertheless the property of the Church of England. 'We know that alteration to the church is not possible,' the proposal continued. 'Therefore, we promise to raise a suitable memorial without harming it.'[clxiii] (One would love to know what plans they would have suggested if alteration to the church had been possible.) The proposal finished with a ringing entreaty: 'in the name of justice and humanness, we appeal to the concerned authorities to respond to the feelings of the Sikhs and allow them to raise a suitable memorial to the Maharajah.'[clxiv]

On returning to India Kulmohan Singh wrote to thank Bone for his help and asked him for news of progress concerning the memorial 'near Elveden church'. The letter, dated 14 May 1992, confirmed that their ambitions went beyond a simple memorial in the churchyard, because he said that his organisation had decided to provide a person who would look after 'that particular museum/library/multi religious centre'.[clxv]

The last letter in the archive from Kulmohan Singh to Bone is a note enclosing a cutting from *The Indian Express*, dated 23 January 1993, which makes it clear that a deputation of Sikhs had recently made an approach to the Elveden estate. The paper reported that plans to erect a statue of Duleep Singh at Elveden Hall 'are being cold-shouldered by the owner, fearing a turbaned invasion.'[clxvi]

In fact, this approach had been made on behalf of British Sikhs by an organisation called the Maharajah Duleep Singh Centenary Trust (referred to as the Trust hereafter), which was founded in 1993 and supported by the Nanaksar Thath Isher Darbar gurdwara in Walsall. This British Trust had no connection with the organisation in New Delhi, whose efforts appear by then to have petered out.

The primary object of the new Trust was to promote Anglo-Sikh heritage and recognition for Duleep Singh, which it felt he had been denied during his lifetime. The Trust was represented by a group of friends that included academics, community leaders and others, but their most energetic and vocal member was Harbinder Singh Rana, a businessman from Walsall, who was born in Punjab in 1960 and brought to Britain when he was three years old. His name was mentioned in almost all the newspaper reports describing the meetings held between the Trust and the other interested parties. Indeed, his vision for the memorial was the one that dominated the proposals made by the Sikhs from 1993 onwards.

The story in *The Indian Express* had been picked up from *The Guardian*, which on 20 January 1993 reported at length on the situation in Elveden. Under the unfortunate if predictable subheading 'statue argy-bhaji', it described Elveden as 'a squirearchical country estate', and called negotiations between the Sikhs and the estate owners a 'clash of cultures'. 'City dwellers in turbans' and callers at the estate office were being told that 'the only public place is the churchyard' and were advised that once they had had a look at the grave the best thing was to continue along the A11.[clxvii] Relations between the two sides had evidently broken down already, with the Elveden estate making it clear that it wanted nothing to do with the Sikhs or their memorial.

It was only natural that the Sikhs would want to see their memorial placed close to the home in which Duleep Singh had spent the greater part of his adult life, where six of his children had been born and brought up. He purchased the Elveden estate in 1863, the year before his marriage, and as we have seen he arranged to have it remodelled while he and his new bride were on their honeymoon in Egypt and Scotland. He employed the architect John Norton, who had been President of the Architectural Association in 1858-59, and had made his career by designing neo-Gothic renovations for parish churches.[clxviii] However, he probably appealed to Duleep Singh because at the time of his Elveden commission he had just completed his designs for Tyntesfield, a house overlooking the Bristol Channel, owned by the guano millionaire William Gibbs, to which an extra floor, two new wings and towers had been added. Norton arranged for this modest Regency house to be swallowed up by a soaring Gothic-revival masterpiece bristling with ornamentation that incorporated pinnacles, gables, crenellated towers, stained glass and leaded-light windows.[clxix] Duleep Singh had no taste for Gothic revivalism, but he was probably impressed by Norton's gift for projecting architectural flights of imagination onto existing buildings. It was Norton's method, not his theology that appealed to him.

The original house at Elveden dated from the mid-eighteenth century and was a pleasant-looking if undistinguished three-storey building of nine bays, built of red brick with stone quoins and a simple porch. Duleep Singh ordered Norton to have the place virtually rebuilt. He lavished huge sums of money on his new home and when the job was done much of the old Hall had been demolished. A whole new wing had been constructed, subsequently called the Maharajah's Wing; a balustrade had been added to the roofline, and the entrance front had been embellished with a portico of two pairs of coupled columns. The frontage was likewise restructured with bay windows, little balconies on the third floor, and Ancaster-stone dressings throughout. Its first owner would not have recognised it. Gone was the country house, suitable for a retired admiral, and in its stead a magnificent palace had arisen, fitting seat for a prince.

Its first owner would have been still more astonished by the interior that Norton had created for his profligate client. *The Builder* reported later that Norton had the 'gratification' of being instructed to decorate the interior 'with pure Indian ornament'. Inspired by photographs taken in India by Samuel Bourne and a collection of watercolours provided by the Maharajah himself, Norton certainly fulfilled his brief. Most of the new principal rooms – the hall, the drawing room on the south front, the dining room and billiard room on the north front – were encrusted with ornamental plasterwork in the Indian style. The hall was especially spectacular, with its fancy arches, mirrored ceilings and magnificent sweeping staircase of polished marble steps and cast-iron balustrade. Its walls were hung with the Maharajah's collection of paintings by the Austrian artist August Schoefft, who had painted Duleep Singh as a child. Among many other paintings on display were a copy of Winterhalter's portrait of Duleep Singh and Schoefft's famous depiction of Ranjit Singh as he listened to a reading of the Sikh holy book with the Golden Temple at Amritsar in the background.

Apart from the columns, which were left white, most surfaces were richly coloured, in some places with coloured cements. The cast-iron balustrade was lacquered sealing-wax red. The central part of the floor in the hall was covered with a huge Indian carpet surrounded by a margin laid with marble and specially made coloured encaustic tiles. In imitation of buildings in Lahore and Delhi, the ceilings were elaborately decorated. The drawing-room ceiling, for example, was gilded and inlaid with stars and crescents of silvered glass as well as a tracery of foliage in mirrors, with bright red berries attached to the mirrored twigs. The panels of arches round the walls were lined with mirrors and the walls themselves were covered with silken hangings, while the room was rendered even more luxurious by its sumptuous furnishings. Gold shawls from

India shimmered on the walls of the library.

In keeping with the profusion inside the house, the gardens were crowded with exotic birds and creatures: 'huge vultures and sleepy-looking eagles were chained to posts; numerous aviaries were full of ostriches, Australian crows, various pigeons, peacocks, and rare birds of many kinds. Kangaroos, cheetahs, or hunting leopards and monkeys were also there.[clxx]

Between them Norton and the Maharajah had created what Nikolaus Pevsner called 'an Oriental extravaganza unparalleled in England'.[clxxi]

During his years of ownership the Maharajah extended the size of his estate by buying up additional land. He was respected as a landlord who kept his properties in good condition, at least during the early years before he had lost interest and run through his money. He restored the Church of St Andrew, which stood within sight of the Hall at the edge of its grounds, and added a vestry and a priest's door. He also donated a large, stained-glass window. His generosity towards the church may be interpreted as a gesture conventionally expected from a wealthy landlord, or it may be a sign of the Maharajah's sincere commitment to Christianity during this period.

Most famously, the Maharajah turned Elveden into a shooting estate, stocked with pheasants, partridges, woodcock, hares and rabbits, where he entertained the rich and aristocratic, including the Prince of Wales, who loved to attend his lavish hunting parties. The Maharajah was himself an excellent shot and achieved several records, one of which is said to stand to this day: on 8 September 1876 he 'bagged' 780 birds with 1,000 cartridges, the largest bag ever made by one gun in England. The Prince of Wales' pleasure in his visit to Elveden is palpable in a letter he wrote to a friend: 'We had the most extraordinary good days shooting having killed yesterday and today close on 6,000 head, nearly 4,500 of which were pheasants! It is certainly the most wonderful shooting I ever saw.'[clxxii]

All this came to an end in 1886, however, when the Maharajah gave instructions for the estate to be put up for rent. By then he had allowed Elveden to fall into neglect. The guns had fallen silent, and the pheasants strutted through the coveys undisturbed. Their owner was only interested in getting what he could for his property in order to finance his trip to the Punjab. In a series of auctions in April and May 1886 the rest of his possessions and the remaining contents of the Hall were sold in his absence, for by then he was detained in Aden. *The Times* took pleasure in reporting how cheaply everything went for. 'Elveden Hall has been so transformed from an old red-brick mansion into a sort of oriental palace, that it would have to be considerably restored back to its English garb to suit most tastes.'[clxxiii] The vindictive tone of the article indicates how far the Maharajah had fallen in popularity since the heady days of his arrival in England as a teenager.

He was never to return to Elveden, except in his coffin. His funeral was attended by many people, including representatives of the Queen and the Prince of Wales, whose wreath bore the message, 'For auld lang syne'. Despite the fact that the Maharajah had made a well-publicised disavowal of Christianity when he was reinitiated into Sikhism in Aden, he was given a Christian funeral service, which was conducted by the rector of St Andrew, and was of 'extreme plainness'. As Christy Campbell wrote, 'The Maharajah Duleep Singh was buried a Christian in a Saxon church laden with the memorials of the great and the good. England had reclaimed him.'[clxxiv] At the very end his connection with Elveden was secured. If he belonged anywhere in England, it was in Elveden, the scene of his glory days, the place of his burial.

(In one small respect his restoration to Christianity was not complete: whereas both his wife's tombstone and his son's bear biblical quotations, Duleep Singh's carries only his name, dates and the places of his birth and death.[clxxv])

The following year Elveden Hall with its estate was purchased by Sir Edward Guinness (who became the 1st Earl of Iveagh in 1919) for £159,000. He too spent a fortune on the place, more than doubling the size of the house by adding a vast servants' wing of 180 rooms. He replaced Duleep Singh's Indian hall with one of his own that rose through four storeys and was surmounted by a cupola with a copper-covered dome. In place of the Maharajah's plasterwork he installed white Carrara marble, also carved in an eclectic style drawing on Indian inspiration. According to Clive Aslet, a special railway line had to be constructed to transport the marble from Burnham Market.[clxxvi] The new Indian hall was in the form of a cross, with an apse and five pairs of French windows opening onto the south-facing terrace. Four arches sprang from the first-floor level to carry the great dome, whose inner face was covered with stylised flowers and vases. The dome and its supporting structures were thick with tracery and marble stalactites.[clxxvii]

Guinness realised his scheme with great thoroughness, spending £70,000 on his version of an Indian palace, and employing 700 craftspeople. Every detail was researched with pedantic care, and the whole enterprise was overseen by Caspar Purdon Clarke, Director of the Victorian and Albert Museum and an expert in Indian decoration. At some point during these refurbishments the brilliant colours that Duleep Singh had favoured were whitewashed.[clxxviii] 'We whitewashed everything, us Guinnesses. It does get dark in winter in Suffolk,' the current Lord Iveagh has said by way of justification.[clxxix] (In the same interview he also referred to the Hall as 'a shooting box – A large shooting box!'[clxxx])

By the time he received his title Lord Iveagh was reckoned to be the second richest man in England. The contents of his house reflected his great wealth: every room was luxuriously appointed and opulently furnished, and the whole collection was 'set off by orchids, palms, flowering plants, and the electric light'. In a word, Elveden was 'an appallingly luxurious mansion,' according to the magazine *Mayfair*.[clxxxi] When it was finished Purdon Clarke proposed an inscription to explain the purpose of the design, which was 'to reproduce, in England, the best examples of Moghul Architecture.'[clxxxii] Clive Aslet, author of *The Edwardian Country House*, describes Iveagh's reconstruction of Elveden as 'an astonishing private monument to the vision of Empire',[clxxxiii] but he also comments that, for all the scholarship devoted to its arches, lantern, copper doors and flowing ribbons of carved marble, the effect on the uninitiated was of a Taj Mahal transported to the heathlands of Suffolk.[clxxxiv]

In the course of thirty years an English country house had provided the humble clay from which two fantastic 'pleasure domes' had been fashioned, one designed by an exiled prince to evoke the Rajput palaces of a lost childhood, the other a fantasy of oriental imperialism conjured up by an Irish multi-millionaire who probably never set foot in India.

Lord Iveagh returned Elveden to its former glory as a shooting estate, and he too entertained the Maharajah's old friend, now King Edward VII, as well as his son, who was to become George V, and his grandson, who was to become George VI. It is said that more pheasants and partridges were shot at Elveden than at any other estate in England. The biggest recorded bag was in 1912, when five guns killed 3,247 birds.[clxxxv]

Lord Iveagh applied his grandiose methods to the church, where he outdid Duleep Singh by attaching another, larger nave to the original, which effectively reduced the old St Andrew to the south aisle of the new edifice. This was a gesture both extravagant and practical, because the new building could accommodate the greatly enlarged staff, for whom attendance was compulsory.

Lord Iveagh also added a new bell tower connected to the church by a long cloister-walk. Pevsner noted, rather disdainfully, that the detail on these additions was in the most ornate style of Art Nouveau Gothic, 'full of unexpected and unauthorized turns.'[clxxxvi]

Lord Iveagh died in 1927, and though his son maintained a shoot on the grounds he was more interested in farming, and under his ownership Elveden became a successful agricultural enterprise. The second Earl died in 1967, but by then the Guinness family had chosen to live elsewhere on the estate, leaving the Hall to be occupied by caretakers only. During the Second World War it was used as a headquarters for the USAAF and suffered considerable damage when the staff quarters were struck and destroyed by a bomb. In 1984 the third Earl Iveagh announced that he would never live in the Hall again, and gave instructions to Christie's to hold what journalists named 'The Sale of the Century',[clxxxvii] disposing of the entire contents of the house, including several items once owned by Duleep Singh. The auction took place in May 1984, and when the final hammer came down at the end of five days of bidding the Hall had been completely emptied. It was then left to stand, unoccupied and deserted. Sikhs and other visitors to the churchyard could wander across the grounds to peer through the windows into the empty rooms.

In 1992 the third Earl died and Arthur Edward Rory ('Ned') Guinness inherited both his title as the fourth Earl and the Elveden estate; he was twenty–one years old. Since then he has lived in Elveden, though not in the Hall.

In 2001 he was married in the church. Today his Elveden property comprises some 22,486 acres of woodland and farmland, on which it is said that ten per cent of the nation's onions are grown.

1992 was also the year the Trust made its application for a memorial to be located somewhere in Elveden. No sooner had the young Earl acquired his title than a deputation of Sikhs came knocking at his door. It was, of course, his prerogative to decide one way or the other about the placing of a memorial on his property, but it would be very interesting to know exactly what the Sikhs proposed. Were they merely asking to raise a statue, or did they hint at something more substantial – a 'museum/library/multi-religious centre' – that would have attracted much larger numbers of visitors than a memorial? (Brian Keith Axel reported that some Sikh entrepreneurs even attempted to buy Elveden Hall, but provided no further details.[clxxxviii])

It is clear from newspaper reports that the Earl and his family, or at any rate the management responsible for the estate, found the Sikhs' proposal, whatever it was, utterly unacceptable. In its account of the story *The Guardian* focussed on the efforts of Elveden's rector, the Reverend Paul Ensor, to mediate between the parties. Many years later Ensor's recall of those mediations was vivid: 'dealing with the Sikhs' determination on the one hand, and Elveden's obstinacy on the other, was like walking on gilded splinters.'[clxxxix] *The Guardian* reported that the rural dean of Thetford had the impression that people in the village thought they were 'under siege'.[cxc]

Part of the estate's hostility to the Sikhs and their proposal was the fear that large numbers of visitors would 'invade' the village if the Trust's plan were put into action, even if it only involved enhancing the graves. In previous years Elveden had been a favourite destination for large numbers of Sikhs travelling from Birmingham, Wolverhampton, Bradford and London, who wanted to pay homage to their last Maharajah at his graveside. These visitors were not hospitably greeted by the villagers. In 1961 a Sikh was discovered praying in the church, an act so disturbing that some parishioners demanded to know if the church would have to be reconsecrated. Thirty years later the community was agitated by different grievances, even if the welcome was no warmer: litter, noise and trespassing on the Hall's grounds were common complaints, and the sight of plastic swords left on the graves gave offence.

The situation in Elveden was sufficiently newsworthy for *The Guardian* to commission a long article by its religious affairs editor, Madeleine Bunting. 'I have to say the Sikhs are a bit of a nightmare,' one villager told her. 'They look rather strange. I suppose we're not used to people like that round here.' (This was something of a contradiction, because it was the numbers of visitors that were provoking the complaints in the first place.) Another villager, whose family was buried in the churchyard, complained to Bunting that the visiting Sikhs 'walk over the other graves and leave plastic swords about. They don't think of others. They take too much on themselves, but they probably think I'm prejudiced. It's not worth putting up a plaque, but it's their prerogative. I've lived here for forty years. It won't bother me. If they have celebrations here, I won't go.'[txci] In the same article Bunting quoted a vicar working in the county, who wrote, 'After twenty years in London and three in East Anglia, the ugliest racism I have met was at the garden gate of a Suffolk cottage, without a single black face in sight.'[txcii]

But, looking back on these events, Ensor was keen to defend his one-time parishioners. In his opinion, the animosity towards the Sikhs did not come from the community, but from the managers of the Elveden estate, most of whom had been appointed by the late third Earl. Bunting passed her own verdict on this wretched affair. 'The coach-loads of Sikh children from Wolverhampton who went to Elveden last summer were thrilled. It's the very Englishness of Elveden which make the story so potent. The wrought iron gates, the empty mansion and the romantic sweep of parkland exert a snobbish fascination. All this once belonged to their co-religionist... But the Sikhs are up against a passive, stubborn, rural brand of British racism.' Since the chief complaint against the Sikhs was that they asked for directions, she tartly suggested that a few signposts wouldn't go amiss.[cxciii]

Elveden in 1993 was an unusual place by the standards of Suffolk villages, because by then most of them had undergone an overlooked revolution in terms of labour and housing, a social revolution with radical consequences. Since the 1970s modern farming had required an increasingly reduced workforce, and landowners had gradually ceased to be the chief employer and landlord in their village. Instead of housing their labourers in tied cottages, farmers were selling off properties to people who were not necessarily local, or renting them to people they did not employ. In some cases, they even leased their land, preferring to harvest rents rather than crops. They remained rich, but their power and influence were greatly diminished.

This had not happened in Elveden, where nothing had changed since Duleep Singh's time; it remained a relic of squirearchy. The village was still in the possession of a single person, now Lord Iveagh, who owned every property (bar one) on the entire estate. He was the chief employer, almost the only employer, and he owned the homes in which his employees lived. His power and influence were undiminished. All village institutions – the church, the school, the post office, the pub and so on – would have felt the weight of his approval or disapproval, no matter how tactfully applied, and since most villagers owed their livelihoods to his discretion, they would have been careful not to incur his disapproval. As Bunting tellingly reported, 'some villagers will only say that they are waiting to see what line the estate takes [regarding the Sikhs' requests] – almost everyone works or used to work for the estate.'[xciv]

In his book *Between Colonialism and Diaspora* Tony Ballantyne argued that by resisting the Sikhs the 'local population [of Elveden] attempted to excise Dalip (*sic*)

Singh from their community memory and protect their vision of Elveden as quintessentially "English".[xcv] The appearance of turbaned interlopers in their village, he maintained, called into question 'an unreconstructed white Protestant Englishness' and manifested cultural differences in ways that 'could not be absorbed into the vision of England cherished by the villagers'.[xcvi] He went on to say that the arrival of the Sikhs in Elveden 'punctured the "peace", predictability, and homogeneity that villagers treasured. The Sikhs were not only visiting Elveden; they were laying claim to its Britishness'.[xcvii]

On their side, the Sikhs were attempting to share 'Britishness' with the British, as the motto of the Trust declared: 'Bringing History and Culture Together'. But there was another dimension to Elveden's suspicion of the Sikhs. Because of its unusual circumstances, Elveden was much less accustomed to 'outsiders' than most other villages in the region, and its villagers were still in the grip of a culture of deference, which was the necessary product of their dependence on a single landlord/employer.[cxviii] They were isolated from the outside world, both protected and imprisoned within their village. They were used to obeying the authority that emanated in the name of the Earl from the estate office. The Sikhs, on the other hand, were attempting to reinstate the posthumous prestige of an alternative: Duleep Singh. They sought to re-invest the abandoned Hall with the spirit of the Maharajah, who in his day had been quite the equal of the Iveaghs in aristocratic status. He too had restructured the Hall, renovated the church, patronised the village, and shot as many birds in the company of as many princes as any Iveagh. No wonder the village waited to hear what the office had to say on the subject of this rival, albeit ghostly authority.

Eight

TO THETFORD

By the spring of 1993 the Maharajah Duleep Singh Centenary Trust had conceded that it could not persuade the Elveden estate to permit a statue or any kind of memorial on private estate land; the Iveagh family was not willing to contemplate the possibility of busloads of Sikhs descending on the village. One member of the Trust recalled with good humour the rebuff the Sikhs had received, but he was well aware of a chauvinist undertow that flowed beneath the mostly polite caution shown to them in the village. 'We did face opposition and I think some of it came from a guilty conscience. We were raking up memories that made both the church and the ruling class uncomfortable.'[cxcix] There were some rare voices in the community that offered a different opinion. A parish councillor said that he was sure there were village organisations that might benefit from money raised by the Sikhs, adding that 'whatever view was taken of the Sikh connection, it remained a part of village history.'[cc] Nevertheless, the Trust was forced to alter its plans.

By way of a compromise the Trust addressed the church, proposing that a 'shelter' or canopy be placed over the graves of Duleep Singh, his wife and son. As it happened, there was a famous precedent for a *chattri*, and that was the war memorial near Brighton and Hove. It stands where a number of Sikh and Hindu soldiers from India, having given their lives on behalf of the British Empire, were cremated during the First World War, but it was not built on consecrated ground.

Sure enough, the church authorities did not like the idea: the graveyard was consecrated, a place of Christian worship. Ensor, the rector, warned that there would have to be 'much discussion' over any proposal affecting the church, and it would certainly involve both the Bishop and the Diocesan Advisory Committee.[cci] The Trust argued that the Sikhs intended nothing sacrilegious: 'We only wanted to make the graves more conspicuous. Our plan was to put a canopy over them, like a *chattri*. We wanted to adorn them with an oriental twist. We didn't want to stir up trouble or make accusations about what happened to Duleep Singh.'

The parish council chairman took a dim view of the whole fracas. 'I can understand the Sikhs, or whatever they call themselves, may wish to celebrate the centenary

… [but] I know very little about Sikhs.[tcii] He need not have worried, because the diocese mostly ruled against the Sikhs, leaving them to console themselves with grudging concessions. The Bishop would not sanction the inter-faith service proposed by the Sikhs, on the grounds that the church must preserve the integrity of Christianity. Graveyard law dictated that canopies over graves, of whatever shape or design, were forbidden. However, a plaque dedicated to Duleep Singh's memory was deemed acceptable, with the possibility that the Bishop himself might graciously unveil it during a service that would be Christian, but to which some members of the Sikh community would be invited. For its part, the estate agreed to allow its carpark to be used for the occasion.[cciii]

And that appeared to bring to an end the much-feared turban invasion of Elveden.

On 11 January 1993 a meeting took place in Thetford that was attended by the Trust and representatives of Forest Heath and Breckland district councils, Thetford Town Council, the University of East Anglia and Blo' Norton Parish council. (Blo' Norton Hall was for many years the home of Prince Frederick, Duleep Singh's second son and a great local benefactor.) 'Black Friar', a correspondent for *The Thetford and Brandon Times*, reported that the Sikhs now had an 'understanding of the delicacy of the

matter and ... wish[ed] to put on a more professional and acceptable footing some of their hopes and activities', which he referred to as their 'great design'. He finished his article with a paragraph that summed up the attitude of the wider local community outside Elveden: 'Cultural and religious differences there may be. But [Duleep Singh] was a significant figure in the history of this region and efforts by his own people to properly mark the fact ought to be given at least a genuine hearing.'[tciv]

This 'great design' was formally unveiled in the shape of a large leaflet issued by the Trust that described the events and activities envisaged for the centenary year. There was no mention of canopies over the graves; instead, the Trust now talked of donating a commemorative plaque to the church in Elveden, and of commissioning a memorial to be placed, not in Elveden, but 'in the Thetford area'. The leaflet announced that 'an open-air festival with performers, musicians and poets etc.' was planned. The Trust also intended to establish a 'research chair' at the University of East Anglia, and it was going to commission a booklet and portraits of the Maharajah. From the outset the Sikhs left no doubt that they intended to foot the bill for all these items, as well as any other forms of celebration.

Under its title 'Bringing History and Cultures Together', the leaflet incorporated a short manifesto, explaining the need for these centenary celebrations. It provided a succinct insight into the way the British Sikh diaspora saw its identity in relation to its colonial past and its current relations with Britain: 'The Maharaja's connection with Britain marked the commencement of an association between the nations which saw Sikh troops serving gallantly in world wars and is today represented by a Sikh community which plays an active and responsible part in British society.' It went on to say that the centenary programme would highlight the historical Anglo-Sikh association and promote future friendship between the two communities, particularly through its East Anglian connection.

It was characteristic of the Sikh mentality, at least in its British form, that the leaflet's authors chose to translate the events of 1849 and Duleep Singh's dethronement, which might have been seen as a colonial humiliation, into 'the commencement of an association between the nations'. Harbinder Singh described the intentions of the Trust at that time: 'Our aim was to draw attention to Duleep Singh, but our strategy contained a bigger mission. Although the Sikhs were a visible minority, whose contribution on the British side to the two world wars was recognised by many people, there was no real understanding of the background to the relationship between Britain and the Sikhs. How had their paths crossed? The Trust thought that the centenary was a great opportunity to revive the Duleep Singh story, but beyond that we wanted to persuade the public to acknowledge that the relationship between Britain and the Sikhs had far deeper historical roots than recent immigration. The centenary celebrations were designed to correct the impression that the Sikhs were people who had just come here by stealth on boats in the 1960s, trying to get asylum. The fact was that every aspect of the Sikhs' destiny – political, religious, military, economic, agricultural and cultural – had been fashioned by Britain from annexation in 1849 to Partition in 1947. The Trust wanted the host community to understand that the status of the Sikhs was not the result of decisions taken in India by them, but of decisions taken by the British authorities in Westminster. It was a narrative that had never been properly told, and the Trust wanted to rectify this while at the same time explaining how Sikh history and Sikh values were inseparable.[ccv]

By May 1993 considerable progress had been made. Plans for the memorial seemed to have become much more ambitious. Under the ringing title 'Memorial square to honour Sikh', *The East Anglian Daily Times* reported that John Wormald, an architect from Edgbaston in Birmingham, had been commissioned to work on designs for a tribute to Duleep Singh, which he believed would be sited on Butten Island in Thetford. 'It will be like a memorial garden or square, with a colonnaded approach leading to a life-sized equestrian statue on a plinth in the middle,' he said. 'It will be a processional route you walk through, for an experience, and although quite modest it will be more than just a statue, but a special place.' Wormald said that the Trust hoped to start building in August, if Breckland District Council planners gave the go-ahead.[ccvi]

The Thetford Times offered a slightly different account of the plans, foreseeing 'an avenue of monoliths' leading to a bronze statue of an 'Indian prince' on horseback, with an accompanying memorial stone to tell the story of Queen Victoria's favourite. It also reported that the Breckland recreation and tourism committee had agreed in principle on Butten Island, a conservation area.[ccvii]

Breckland's leisure manager told the paper that thousands of Sikhs were expected to flock to Thetford in the summer for the memorial celebrations. His attitude to this prospect struck a refreshing note of anticipation. 'Elveden's loss', he said, 'is our gain. Thetford and Breckland together will benefit immensely from this cultural event.'[ccviii] And that note, which might be described as one of hospitable commercialism, has more or less characterised Thetford and Breckland Council's attitude towards the Sikhs ever since.

A memorial square, a colonnade, an equestrian statue – these elements may have been in the minds of the Sikhs all along, but this was the first time that the public were made aware of the scale and grandeur of the projected Duleep Singh memorial. So too was the fact that it would be located in Thetford, on Butten Island.

Ever since Duleep Singh's time in Elveden a connection had existed between the Sikhs and the district, which was cemented by the generosity of his second son, Prince Frederick (1868-1926), who had also lived in the area, though in humbler circumstances. Among other gifts, Frederick gave the town the Ancient House, now its museum. But it was not until these discussions in the early 1990s about the centenary monument that the British Sikh community at large and the people of Thetford made a friendship that was to prove both enduring and convivial. The friendship was all the more remarkable because the great majority of Sikh immigrants had settled in parts of England, such as London and the Midlands, that were a long way from Norfolk, while Thetford itself had never had more than a handful of Sikh residents. The Sikhs were to be admired for their willingness to travel large distances to reach Thetford, a town which for much of its history had not been a destination for tourists; and Thetford, for its part, was to be commended for welcoming the Sikhs. So far from seeing them as a 'turbaned invasion', Thetford celebrated its unlikely association with these exotic visitors.

Nine
BUTTEN ISLAND

This excursion is largely for the benefit of those who have never visited Thetford – unlucky people – for whom the town, if they have heard of the place at all, may indeed be a byword for botched urban development and social anomie. The significance of Butten Island, and its perfect aptness as a site for the Duleep Singh statue, cannot be fully appreciated without knowing a little about Thetford's long, but mostly uneventful history.[ccix]

As with so many ancient communities, Thetford owes its existence and its name to geography, for it stands at a place where the River Thet can be forded, which also happens to be the point where it converges with the much longer Little Ouse. The bigger river connected the town with the Great Ouse and the North Sea in one direction, and the heart of England (Northamptonshire, Buckinghamshire, Bedfordshire, Cambridgeshire) in the other.

During the Roman and early Saxon periods the community that occupied this area was mostly agricultural, but in due course a large town established itself, occupying 200 acres on either side of the river. By the Norman Conquest Thetford had become the sixth largest town in England, ranking in size with Norwich, Oxford and Lincoln, despite having been sacked twice by the Danes. According to the Domesday census its population in 1066 was about 4,500 people.

If Thetford had a golden age it was in the eleventh century. In 1071 Bishop Herfast, a Norman appointment, moved his see from Elmham to Thetford, elevating the Church of St Mary to cathedral status, and the city seemed to face a future bright with power and prosperity. But it was not to be. In 1094, a mere twenty-three years later, a new Bishop moved his throne to Norwich, and Thetford fell into decline. Its surrounding farmland became relatively infertile; its market fell victim to the aggressive energy of its competitors, particularly Bury St Edmunds; and its pottery business failed, leaving the town without a staple industry.

Despite the loss of the Bishop's seat, medieval Thetford remained a significant religious centre, and by the early fifteenth century, with a population reduced to around 1,500, it was the home of no fewer than five religious houses and several other monastic hospitals and hostels. The largest was the Cluniac Priory, founded in 1103, which became nationally famous as a place of pilgrimage after the Virgin Mary was said to have appeared in a vision, requesting the addition of a lady chapel. During its construction, a cache of relics was uncovered which included the winding sheet of Lazarus, a most fortunate discovery that turned Thetford into a nationally famous place of pilgrimage and greatly improved its economy. However, by the early fourteenth century the monks had mismanaged their affairs so badly that the King was obliged to take the destitute priory under his protection.

In 1540, the priory was forced to 'surrender' as part of Henry VIII's dissolution of the monasteries, and Thetford lost its only significant asset. Over the next three centuries its buildings were gradually dismantled, providing a free source of materials for local builders to ransack. So little remained that in 1845 the Eastern Counties Railway considered siting its station among the few remaining ruins.[ccx] In the event, the station was built further north, and the priory grounds were saved to give Thetford's people a much-needed public space close to the centre that was both beautiful and a poignant reminder of the town's medieval prestige. Thus, a parallel can be seen between Thetford's need to reclaim its few treasures from the past, and the Sikhs' corresponding desire to reclaim Duleep Singh from the forgetfulness of imperial history.

It has to be said that very few noteworthy events punctuated the decrepit torpor in which Thetford languished during the five centuries that elapsed after the destruction of its religious houses. Queen Elizabeth I paid a royal visit in 1578, an honour that sank the impoverished town still further into debt. Thomas Paine was born in Thetford in 1837 and educated in its grammar school, but he wasted no time in leaving the place as soon as he was old enough. Thetford subsequently repaid the compliment by showing a marked lack of enthusiasm when in 1964 the idea of raising a statue in the great revolutionary's honour was proposed.

In Paine's day Thetford was synonymous with corruption; indeed, it was said to be the rottenest of the rotten boroughs. By then it was an assize town, and it was also notorious for the horrific conditions in which prisoners were held prior to their trials, and for the brutality with which they were executed afterwards on Gallows Hill. Its health record was appalling, with a death rate from epidemics that was worse in the mid-1880s than London's Whitechapel, haunt of Jack the Ripper, a disgrace that was hardly surprising since the town did not have a proper sewerage system until the 1930s.

The town was occasionally roused from its economic inertia by local industries, such as the manufacture of pulp ware and the production of Burrell's steam engines, but it remained a severely depressed town into the mid-twentieth century. But then, in 1957, it became the subject of a revolution; not the kind of revolution favoured by Thomas Paine, but a radical social upheaval all the same. Under the Town Development Act of 1952, Thetford signed up for an expansion scheme that provided for the construction of sufficient houses to accommodate 5,000

Londoners. At that time its population was roughly what it had been at Domesday. The transplantation of these Londoners, unflatteringly described as 'overspill', was accompanied by a small economic boom. Factories engaged in light industry gave work to the new residents, and unemployment dropped to below three per cent in 1975. It is no exaggeration to say that Thetford's population exploded: by 1986 there were 21,000 people living in the town, which had grown faster than any other town in England and Wales, racking up an astonishing increase between 1951 and 1981 of 441 per cent. It had now become the fourth largest town in Norfolk, a status it had not enjoyed since the twelfth century.[ccxi] However, this dramatic expansion did not induce harmonious social relations: the old and new communities regarded each other with mutual dislike, and the town soon acquired a reputation for crime and aggression.

The 1980s saw a return to a more familiar depression, as wages fell, unemployment returned, and several large employers closed or shrank their work forces. By then the town's centre had been redeveloped (ominous word) to provide shopping facilities for its enlarged population, and many buildings described by Thetford's historian, Alan Crosby, as 'unimpressive but attractive and historic', had been torn down.[ccxii] Among the uglier products of this development were the shopping precincts incorporating parts of King Street and Tanner Street. Flint buildings, some of them dating from Elizabethan times and earlier, were torn down to make way for a row of shops, whose unbecoming rear entrances were staggered along the river's edge, leaving an empty area paved with concrete slabs and furnished with a few metal benches. This was the town's idea of a riverfront plaza. It is true that the Borough Council laid out parks and gardens along the river bank, and cleaned the river itself, but instead of beautifying the south bank opposite the Bell Hotel, the council utilised the site as a bus station and carpark. What a wasted opportunity!

However, the planners did get one thing right, and that was Butten Island.

There is always something intrinsically appealing about a river frontage, that potentially dramatic interface where human ambition and natural power must find an accommodation. In Thetford's case, the topography of its waterway is unusually interesting. Flowing from the south, the Little Ouse takes a north-westerly turn as it approaches the town and for a few hundred yards runs parallel with its tributary, the River Thet, which rises only a few miles away. Like a couple with a rendezvous, the two come so close to flowing together that they can be crossed by a single bridge. Then, as if changing their minds about their tryst, the two streams separate again and run side by side before finally getting together just upstream from town's main bridge. This flirtatious little bifurcation on the part of the two rivers has the effect of creating the sliver of land that is known as Butten Island.

Butten Island is roughly 600 feet long and 100 feet wide and, seen from above when its many trees were in full leaf, it would resemble a hairy, green caterpillar. The hand of the planner has intervened with blessed restraint, for the island has mostly been put down to lawn, shaded by trees, with a plain path bordering the bank that faces the Thet. It is a beautiful spot, and it was here that, between them, the Trust, Breckland Council and Thetford Council decided that Duleep Singh's memorial statue should stand – an ideal choice.

TEN

CENTENARY CELEBRATIONS

In July 1993 *The Thetford Times* informed its readers that 'an international open-air festival' for 3,000 Sikhs would be taking place in August, which would bring 'a touch of the East' to the town. Musicians, poets and performers would be travelling from India and visitors would be treated to Punjabi folk dances and Indian refreshments. Entry to the event, which would held at the Breckland Leisure Centre, would be free. The police had been in contact with the organisers to ensure the event went smoothly. 'We are aware that it is an ethnic event – something we are not used to in Norfolk, let alone Thetford,' commented Chief Inspector Martin Wynne in stalwart tones. 'But I am not anticipating any problems.'[ccxiii]

By then it was evident that Duleep Singh's memorial statue, which had yet to be commissioned, would not be ready for either the summer festival or the ceremonies that would mark the date of his death in October. However, *The Thetford Times* reported that plans for the monument would be on show at the festival, and that the statue would be erected the following year – a prediction that proved to be optimistic.

The Trust had approached Elveden estate with the idea of holding the festival in the grounds of the Hall, only to be snubbed a second time. Speaking on behalf of the Trust, Harbinder Singh told the paper that the Elveden estate office had given no reason for 'its resistance to the celebrations'. For once he lost his customary sang-froid: 'It's a bit like the Queen without Buckingham Palace, but Elveden's loss is Thetford's gain. They seem to have a phobia about people coming to the village. We are not a bunch of illiterates from some banana republic. Most of us were born and educated at university here.'[tcxiv]

Paul Ensor recalls that the Elveden estate office was anxious about the prospect of Sikh visitors to the village on the day of the festival. He advised the estate management that the numbers were likely to be large, but they brushed his warnings aside. Requests for coaches to park on estate land were refused. The question of national security must have been raised, because a representative of the Home Office attended some of the meetings. (A security threat was not as far-fetched as it might sound today – see Chapter 6.) The management was more concerned with incursions on the estate and there was talk of stationing groundsmen on all the fences near the graveyard with broken shotguns over their arms. 'That was the level of antipathy,' Ensor remembers.[ccxv]

The response of the Breckland and Thetford Councils was very different. The Mayor of Thetford, Kathy Key, promised to attend the festival in her official capacity. 'It's a great honour for us to have the festival here and it's very good for the future of the [Breckland Leisure Centre].' A representative of the Centre said, 'We have never had anything as grand as this before.'[ccxvi]

The Sikhs' summer festival in Thetford took place on Sunday, 1 August 1993. By all accounts it was a most enjoyable event. The sun shone, and as *The Thetford Times* put it, 'Five thousands Sikhs brought an early Indian summer to Thetford on Sunday with an open-air festival of vibrant colours, exotic fragrances and ethnic music.'[ccxvii] Punjabi folk dancers, Indian musicians and a display of martial arts entertained the biggest crowd the leisure centre had yet seen. People took off their shoes and wore headscarves before entering a makeshift temple in a marquee, where there was a display of memorabilia relating to Duleep Singh. Local dignitaries, who were issued with ceremonial swords, attended a religious service, though many of them found it difficult to sit cross-legged. Speeches and presentations were made, anthems were sung by Sikh college students, and great quantities of Punjabi food were consumed. In Ensor's words, 'the chaos of Amritsar had come to a playing field in Thetford.'

The Mayor pronounced herself delighted. Harbinder Singh said that 'class, colour and religion are irrelevant when you have the same values of hard work and decency.' A former leader of Norwich City Council said that she had a special place in her heart for the Sikh community after visiting Delhi. A resident said that it was a good experience for Thetford because 'round here you don't get much contact with different cultures.' Ensor said the event had been a joy to experience. The manager of the leisure centre said that it was a great pleasure for the centre to host the occasion. And the police said that there had been no trouble, though several residents had asked for the music to be turned down. All in all, the day was a triumph and everyone went home satisfied.[ccxviii]

Ensor's predictions were fulfilled in Elveden. A single policeman on a motorbike had been dispatched to handle the traffic, and he was soon forced to call for assistance. By eleven o'clock the A11 approach to the village was gridlocked. However, no groundsmen with broken shotguns were deployed.

148

The Trust could congratulate itself on having organised a most successful day, but now it had to turn its attention to marking Duleep Singh's death on 22 October. The day was to be commemorated with two events: the unveiling of the plaque at Elveden church, promised to them by the Bishop, and a reception at Breckland House in Thetford, headquarters of Breckland District Council, where plans for the monument on Butten Island would be displayed. In addition the Ancient House Museum planned to hold a centenary exhibition under the title 'East Anglia's Indian Prince and Princesses'.

As part of the centenary celebrations the Trust had commissioned two portraits of Duleep Singh, one by the Sikh artist, Acchar Singh, and the other by the British artist, Anthea Durose. This pairing was consistent with the ideology of the centenary commemorations, which ensured that in every respect the cultures and histories of the Sikhs and the British were projected as equal partners. These two portraits were also on display at the reception in Breckland House.

Durose was a Suffolk painter well known for her skill with portraiture likenesses. Her brief had stipulated only that her portrait should show the Maharajah in a turban; the choice of image to copy was left to her. She selected a steel engraving from the period, but was then faced with the problem of colouring a painting derived from a black-and-white image. She chose to render the Maharajah's suit, which appeared to be made of velvet, in a rich shade of garnet. The pearls that decorated the turban and were wrapped in ropes round her subject's neck caused her great trouble, since she was determined to depict them exactly equal in size. After seeing a preliminary sketch, the Trust asked her to make Duleep Singh appear older, which she did by filling out his face, though without inflating it into the jowly dimensions of his middle age. The Trust also asked her to add a ring to his right middle finger, enclosing a drawing of what was required – a Sikh motif.

The original steel engraving by D. J. Pound had placed the seated figure against a plain grey background, but Durose decided to suggest the ornate style of Elveden's plasterwork by introducing some white pillars and part of an arch to act as a frame. Behind the Maharajah she painted a more or less abstract composition of blueish sky and nebulous clouds, an echo of the Winterhalter portrait. In this way her picture unwittingly reinforced the impression of deracination, of belonging neither in India nor Norfolk, that the Victorian work had initiated, and which became an all-too literal theme in the Maharajah's life.

On the morning of 22 October, before the reception at Breckland House, a sombre ceremony took place at Elveden. To mark the centenary of Elveden Hall's illustrious and controversial resident, a plaque was installed in his memory on the north wall of St Andrew and St Patrick's Church. The carved inscription stated that the plaque was given by the Sikhs of the United Kingdom in memory of Duleep Singh, and it repeated the Trust's motto: Bringing History and Cultures Together.

It rained, but the audience of 'turbaned Sikhs and raincoated local people clutching umbrellas', as *The Thetford Times* described them, was undeterred. It was an occasion for reassuring platitudes, which were perhaps both necessary and fitting, given that the ceremony took place within a stone's throw of the Elveden estate office. Ensor conducted the service and hailed the Maharajah as a symbol of unity. He did at least point out that it was a contradiction for a Sikh leader to be buried in a quiet Suffolk church, but then added that the Maharajah himself had been a mixture of contradictions.[ccxix]

The plaque was not what the Sikhs had really wanted. In Ensor's words, it was a 'sop' from the church, which they had been forced to accept as a poor consolation for having been denied the memorial in Elveden they had originally dreamed of. However, whether they realised it or not at that moment, Elveden estate had done them a good turn, because as events would later confirm Butten Island was a far more suitable site for Duleep Singh's statue.

ELEVEN

A HORSE FOR THE MAHARAJAH

'To rule is to ride.'
Carl Schmitt

'A horse! a horse! my kingdom for a horse!'
Richard III, Act 5, Scene 4

Long before October 1993 it had been obvious to the Trust that the monument, whatever form it took, was not going to be ready for the centenary date. However, another significant date, perhaps the most important one in the Sikh calendar of commemoration, was approaching, and that was 1999, the 300th anniversary of the creation of the *khalsa* in 1699 by the tenth Guru, Gobind Singh.

The Trust had a new target, which gave it some breathing space, and this probably explains why everything went quiet for a year or two.

By a fortunate coincidence 1999 was also an important date for Thetford, because it would mark 800 continuous years of mayoralty. The town had ambitious plans for celebrating the event.

When seeking permission to place the statue on Butten Island, the Trust did not face serious opposition, but it did have to contend with suspicion and incomprehension. It was a steep learning curve on both sides. For the Sikhs the discussions were rendered more difficult by the fact that they had to make long, and in those days difficult, journeys from London and the Midlands to attend meetings in Norfolk. Opinion in Thetford was divided: certain individual councillors were receptive, others were cautious. But, in any case, the Trust soon discovered that planning decisions did not lie with Thetford Council, but with Breckland Council, and persuading their members was 'an uphill struggle'. Whereas most people in Thetford knew something about Duleep Singh and his son Prince Frederick, and were keen to promote their historical connections with the town, people living in Swaffham or Dereham or other areas represented by Breckland had no idea who they were.

Initially, neither the town nor Breckland favoured Butten Island as the location for the statue. The churchyard of St Mary's, a disused church, was suggested, but the Trust rejected the idea, determined that the statue should stand in the heart of Thetford on Butten Island, the location that had originally been proposed in 1993. Butten Island was not only centrally placed, but it was tranquil and free of buildings. As the mayor of the day pointed out, Butten Island was the confluence of two rivers, and in the same way Thetford had become the confluence of two cultures.

The Trust's application was greatly assisted by the architect, John Wormald, who was sympathetic to the Sikhs' aspirations and had an understanding of the historical context. However, on the day of the full planning hearing Harbinder Singh felt he needed to make a persuasive speech if the committee was to be swayed in the Trust's favour. As he remembered it, he asserted that the Trust was trying to raise a monument to someone very important to the Sikhs, a character who was also difficult to erase from the history of East Anglia. He reminded the committee that Duleep Singh's son, Prince Frederick, Thetford's great benefactor, had served in France with the Norfolk Yeomanry during the First World War. Flying on the wings of oratory, he offered a further argument that can never have been heard before in a planning application. He told the committee that even though Duleep Singh was penniless when his tutor, Sir John Login, died in Felixstowe in 1863, he had not hesitated to raise money for his tombstone. If the Maharajah could do that for someone who had converted him to Christianity and deprived him of his liberty, then surely the Sikhs and Breckland should get together to do something for him, to honour his memory?

Who could resist such eloquence?

In May 1997 Breckland Council's Recreation and Tourism Committee finally decided against proposing alternative sites and backed the original plan from 1993 to locate the memorial on Butten Island. Councillors placed a proviso on their agreement, which was that the Trust should be responsible for the upkeep of 'the picturesque site'. The councillors were also concerned that its isolated position might make it a target for vandals, but they were reassured that a CCTV camera placed on the bridge would provide security coverage. As usual, Thetford's approach to the statue was a mixture of hospitality and commercialism. 'It is all part of what Thetford people would like to see in the town,' said one councillor. 'I believe it will bring a lot of tourism to the town.'[tcxx]

In August 1997 it was reported that the Trust had found the necessary funding and was submitting new designs for the site. Harbinder Singh recalls that the money needed to pay for the statue and its plinth was raised very quickly among the Sikh community in the West Midlands and elsewhere, another sign of Duleep Singh's continuing importance to the Sikh diaspora. The Mayor-Elect, Ray Key, was positively welcoming. 'We're very much in favour of having a memorial to the Maharajah in Thetford and we feel very privileged that the trust has agreed to have it here. We're looking forward to it very much.'[tcxxi]

And yet at this point a sculptor had not been commissioned. A sculptor called Denise Dutton had been recommended to Harbinder Singh and he had telephoned her out of the blue in 1995 or 1996, but had not taken the matter any further. However, when the funding became available in 1997 he contacted her again and offered her the commission.

Born in 1964, Dutton was brought up and educated in Bedford. She remembers that she used to play with mud from the River Ouse and make models, and from childhood onwards she had always loved to draw horses. Her education ended without her taking many exams, and she faced an uncertain future at a time when unemployment was high. A career in art did not seem a good idea, so she tried to run her own business, selling models of small animals at craft fairs. One day she saw an advertisement in a paper for sculpture courses at the Sir Henry Doulton School of Sculpture in Stoke-on-Trent, an institution that has since closed. She heard that one of the students was modelling a life-sized horse at the School and decided that was where she wanted to study. After a foundation course in Cambridge, she enrolled as a student in 1990, aged twenty-seven. She was part of the School's third intake and she studied there for three years. She chose the course because she was eager to make 'proper Renaissance-style sculpture,' as she put it, 'and there wasn't a lot of it about in those days.'[tcxxii]

The School was a stand-alone institution funded by industry, with Elizabeth Frink as its patron. Dutton studied life modelling once a week and life drawing once a week, and was left to pursue her own interests during the remaining three days. She studied veterinary anatomy in Cambridge and dissection at King's College Hospital in London. There was no written work on the course, and no exams, but the work was demanding, with three years of study broken by only five weeks' holiday. She loved it. 'I can't praise the course enough. It was the best thing I ever did,' she recalled.[ccxxiii]

The college arranged exhibitions in London and in Lichfield, and Dutton's work was seen by someone who mentioned her name to Harbinder Singh. She seemed especially suitable to the Trust because she had studied equine anatomy and she understood how to combine figures and horses, an ability that had become rare. However, the timing of Harbinder Singh's approach in 1997 did not seem propitious, because she had just broken her wrist after falling off a horse. She recalled that she went for an interview with him in Walsall, and that shortly after that he confirmed that the funding was in place. It was to be her first large-scale commission.

The terms of her agreement with the Trust were not written down, but she was willing to rely on a verbal agreement: she was offered a fee of £11,000 with a deadline of August 1998, when the statue was due to be displayed in Thetford, prior to its official unveiling the following year. She was concerned about her wrist, which had been in a cast since July. The broken bone would not easily knit together, and she was undergoing extensive treatment. Nevertheless, after consulting her doctor and consultant, she began work on the statue around 5 December 1997. No doctor would have prescribed it, but building a life-sized horse figure turned out to be the best therapy for her wrist she could have chosen.

As with Anthea Durose, the Trust gave her a loose brief, which apart from a couple of specific demands, left the initiative with her. The Trust was quite clear that it wanted a life-sized equestrian statue in bronze: 'a hero on horseback'. However, it did not have a particular model in mind for her to follow; instead, it gave her a photograph of the Winterhalter portrait. As a result she thought that the Trust wanted the figure to be extravagantly dressed in his silk costume, and she made a maquette to match the picture. But she was then told that the Trust wanted the figure to have a modern look, and she was given a particular coat to copy. The Trust also requested that the figure should wear a sash round the waist, though Dutton was left free to buy the silk for the sash herself.

The Trust was keen for the face of the statue to bear some likeness to Duleep Singh, albeit at his most handsome and heroic. 'When it came to the statue, we took various liberties,' Harbinder Singh acknowledged. 'His is not the face that contemporary pictures show. The figure that you see in the statue is our romanticised notion: the Duleep Singh that would have been, should have been. We faced some artistic criticism, quite rightly. But we said our mission was to correct history. This is how Duleep Singh should be remembered by future generations of Sikhs and by visitors. That's what we're doing when we show him in that idealised, romantic version. That was our brief to Denise, and we were unanimous over it.[tcxxiv] He added that she was a 'delight' to work with.

Dutton was forced to work with limited reference material. This was in the days before the internet was available, and before the publication of Peter Bance's book *Sovereign, Squire & Rebel* (2009), with its treasure trove of pictures and photographs, but she did find a few useful photographs, including one that was only a photocopy. The Trust wanted her to depict Duleep Singh as a mature man, but she recalled looking at a photograph of Duleep Singh taken outside Elveden Hall, showing him with his 'shooting buddies'; he was 'huge', and the image was therefore unusable. The face she finally sculpted was 'a romanticised version', and was largely based on a photograph taken of him at Osborne House in 1854 when he was sixteen.

Dutton made some preliminary sketches and modelled a quarter-size version before starting work on her life-sized statue. Knowing that the statue would stand on a high plinth, she put her armature on a base, which allowed her to lie on the floor and judge how the statue would look when finally in place. She built her model of horse and rider round the armature, and by surrounding the work with a cage, she was able to 'plumb' the entire structure to make sure that horse and rider were in the right position and properly balanced.

Time was short and she could not afford to make mistakes. Harbinder Singh maintained her morale. She recalled that he had a very good sense of humour. 'He used to telephone me. There were no mobiles in those days, and if I was working on top of the scaffolding I would have to climb all the way down to answer the phone. Then he'd tell me some awful joke and put the phone down. I'd have to go all the way back up again. He was very amusing.'

As with the figure, the horse and its stance was left to Dutton; the Trust did not suggest a precedent from either European or Indian sculpture for her to follow. From illustrations she was familiar with the great equestrian statues of the classical era and the Renaissance, and in particular she was a great admirer of the statue of Gattamelata by Donatello in Padua (1453) and the war memorial in Galashiels by Thomas J. Clapperton (1925).

However, she did not have a particular example in mind when she began work and, as she acknowledged, she had never seen pictures of the equestrian statues in Amritsar of Ranjit Singh, Jassa Singh Ramgarhia, or the Sikh General Attariwala Sham Singh that stands near the India Gate. (Nor, by the way, did she pay any attention to the symbolic position of the hooves said to be favoured by some American and British sculptors: for example, a rearing horse with both front legs in the air indicates that the rider died in battle; one raised front leg signifies that the rider was wounded in battle or died of battle wounds; all four hooves on the ground would mean that the rider died in peacetime.)

160

Dutton's only concern was that the horse should be 'lively', and for that reason she chose to depict a light, athletic sort of horse that would best convey the Trust's vision of the Maharajah. Since Duleep Singh's adult behaviour was seldom heroic, it was as well that she was not familiar with the story of his life. She knew that he had owned Elveden Hall, where she once attended a dinner, and that he had been a great shot, but she had not seen his grave. She was content to fulfil the Sikhs' request: 'He was a hero to them, and that is what they wanted.'

Her work went well, but around Easter 1998 she got into difficulties when trying to model the turban authentically, so she sought guidance from the Trust. Thirteen Sikh men, all wearing turbans themselves, came to her studio, where they gave her thirteen sets of conflicting advice, which she attempted to follow. The next morning, when she looked at the product of their collective guidance, she knew it was a mess, lacking any kind of sculptural shape. She telephoned Harbinder Singh in despair. Ever the pragmatist, he reassured her by telling her to ignore her advisers and do as she thought fit. The result was a turban that seemed to please everyone.

She felt more confident when she came to render the Maharajah's beard. Ignoring the clean-shaven young man in the Osborne photograph, she grafted a full beard onto the Maharajah's face, and continued to work on it, giving it a thick texture and magnificent length. By the time she had finished, it had assumed what she called 'Methuselah' dimensions. A deputation of Sikhs, all bearded themselves, inspected it with admiration, but were forced to rule that it was not an authentic Sikh beard, and she was obliged to trim it back.

She copied the pearls and jewellery that had decorated Duleep Singh's turban and costume in the Winterhalter portrait. She bought plastic pearls from charity shops and constructed the centrepiece attached to the turban from other bits of costume jewellery. Following Winterhalter, she attached the miniature portrait of Queen Victoria to the pearls round the Maharajah's neck, but she broke with precedent by putting a large jewel on an armband round his left sleeve – a decoration more reminiscent of Ranjit Singh and his Koh-i-noor than Duleep Singh.

She made all the equine accoutrements herself, taking especial trouble over the buckles, and was determined to make the harness historically accurate. She consulted the Victoria and Albert Museum, where she was shown some Indian ceremonial harness from the nineteenth century, which she replicated as closely as she could. 'Everything was the way it would have been,' she claimed. She wanted to add a plume to the horse, but Harbinder Singh ruled it out. While she was always eager to add period details, he was only concerned with the heroic appearance of the work. He discouraged her from doing too much research, and told her to put the Winterhalter portrait out of her mind. What he was hoping for was an amalgam of the historical and the modern: the contemporary riding coat combined with the Maharajah's original jewels.

Insofar as she had a particular horse in mind as a model, it was the horse that had caused her to fall and break her wrist, an Anglo-Arab gelding, with light features and a graceful shape. Using many photographs of this animal, she endeavoured to keep it nimble and to give it what she thought of as an oriental feel. She designed the statue so that the vivacity of the piece was generated by the horse more than the man; she wanted an 'organic movement' to pass through the whole structure.

While she was at work on the statue she had no contact with Thetford or Breckland, nor with Oliver Bone at the museum; the statue was an all-Sikh affair. However, John Wormald, the architect, came to her studio; he was wearing a long flowing green coat, which her clay had turned red by the time he left, but he did not involve her in either the design of the site or the installation of the statue.

She needed to locate a foundry capable of handling a piece so large, and she counted herself lucky that she was put in touch with the Castle Fine Arts foundry near Oswestry. The foundry had opened for business a couple of years earlier, and in those days was operating in an old cowshed. Their quote was reasonable (£30,000), and they had a reputation for keeping their deadlines. However, in order to meet the August deadline set by the Trust and give the foundry enough time to work on the moulding, waxes, casting and fettling (trimming and smoothing), Dutton virtually lived in her studio, devoting herself to the statue from December 1997 to May 1998 and often working fourteen hours a day. During the winter months it was very cold and snow would come through the roof, dislodged by crows roosting somewhere above her in the eaves. Her task was demanding because the statue contained many tiny details, and she was concerned that it should be 'spot-on.' 'In the end I was just sitting on the floor in a state of befuddlement, I had been working so long.' She regrets the urgency: 'It was a shame. Another week would have made a difference to me as an artist.' She was still shaping the horse's tail, having worked all through the night, when the foundry came to the studio to make a mould of her model. Even then her work was not done, and she travelled to the foundry to put finishing touches to the statue before it was finally cast in bronze.

Looking back on the experience, she reflected that it was good for her career, for it was a major piece. 'I have wonderful memories of those months; I thought I was the luckiest person in the world.' Her real passion was for statues with figure and horse combined, and she was lucky to be offered what she considered a once-in-a-lifetime chance at the beginning of her career.

(Dutton continued to work, and horses remained her favourite subject.[ccxxv] Among her best-known commissions are a life-sized statue of Amberleigh House, winner of the 2004 Grand National; the horse that carries the Fine Lady Upon a White Horse in Banbury, unveiled by Princess Anne in 2005; and a tribute to the Women's Land Army and Women's Timber Corps that stands in the National Memorial Arboretum in Alrewas, Staffordshire and was unveiled in 2014.)

At the end of January 1998 a wooden cut-out of the statue was unveiled on its prospective site in Thetford. Local officials responsible for the project met at Butten Island and it was reported that although Breckland councillors enthusiastically supported the idea of the statue, they still wanted to gain a clearer idea of how the monument as a whole would look. The Trust hoped to submit plans for the design of the site soon.[ccxxvi]

Dutton and the foundry delivered on time, which enabled the Trust to exhibit the new statue, without its plinth, at the Breckland Leisure Centre in Thetford on Sunday, 30 August 1998. As before, the event attracted a large number of Sikhs; one paper estimated the crowd was 4,000 strong, while another hysterically doubled that figure.[ccxxvii] Dutton came with her family; 'Sikhs love a party,' she recalled. Representatives from the Victoria and Albert Museum also joined the festival, which was free to all comers. The statue, swathed in yellow and blue cloth, was uncovered in front of the crowd and dozens of pink, yellow and blue balloons were released, floating over the bemused town that was once again playing host to Sikh festivities. There were the customary performances of music, poetry readings and displays of martial arts, and on this occasion the Sikhs' contribution to British military history was given prominence, with many Sikh veterans attending. 'They are great role model for how the communities can get on,' Harbinder Singh commented.[ccxxviii]

The town's representatives struck a familiar note of hospitality salted with commercial hard-headedness. The statue was acknowledged as a gift from the Sikh community to the people of East Anglia. The Mayor, Derek Serjeant, stated that he believed the statue would bring more Sikh visitors to the town, while Breckland Council's chairman said the festival would be good for international relations and mutual respect for both cultures.[ccxxix]

What was missing from the reports of this merry jamboree was any assessment of the statue itself as a work of art. There was no question that the Sikhs were pleased with Dutton's work, and it seems to have been well received by Thetford's officials and its residents. It is perhaps surprising that everything turned out so well, because the enterprise had an amateurish, makeshift quality: after all, the sculptor was inexperienced, with no knowledge of either Sikh statuary or Sikh history, or even much knowledge of Duleep Singh's story. None of this mattered to her patrons, who were likewise ignorant of, or uninterested in, the traditions of equestrian sculpture in Europe and India. They simply wanted a statue of their hero, heroically presented on a well-modelled horse, and as it worked out they could not have been luckier in their choice of sculptor.

The figure on the horse had no authenticity as a historical portrait, but then the statue was bound to depart from a literal likeness of its subject. It was impossible to depict a Sikh hero without a beard, turban and sword, the fundamental badges of Sikh religious and national identity, but in Duleep Singh's case these badges had lost their significance. The statue's handsome face with its fine beard and curled mustachios, on which Dutton had lavished so much devotion, bore no likeness to Duleep Singh, who for most of his adult life favoured a moustache and mutton-chop sideboards that left his chin beardless. He only wore his turban for ceremonial occasions and sometimes when having his photograph taken. In any case, it was an empty symbol – literally so – for he had never regrown his hair since cutting it off as a teenager in Fatehgarh. The fact was that the historical Duleep Singh did not possess many of the required attributes of a Sikh hero: he had abandoned Sikhism in favour of Christianity, and once in England he gradually shed the other signs of his ethnic origin by adopting the appearance and behaviour of an English aristocrat. His Sikh clothes became a kind of fancy dress, which he put on for ceremonial and court occasions to please the Queen. Paradoxically, the only truly authentic features of the statue are the charity-shop jewels that adorn her figure, for he never lost his love of jewellery and ornamentation. Dutton was right to incorporate the miniature portrait of Queen Victoria that Winterhalter had made so prominent in his portrait. It remained a consistent badge of the Maharajah's identity, which was both an icon of his father's royal power and an amulet that kept him safe within the Queen's protection.

Powerful men had been depicted on horseback since classical times; the more powerful the horse, the more powerful the man. The combination of horse and rider was an eloquent symbol of domination; when a man sat on a horse, he was elevated above other people, rendering him superior in every sense. In royal iconography the king demonstrated his authority over his subjects through his control over the animal beneath him. As Richard of Gloucester knew all too well, a dismounted king on the battlefield was a defeated king: 'A horse! a horse! my kingdom for a horse!' he cried, before being slain at Bosworth. The art of horsemanship was more than a courtly accomplishment for monarchs; it was a potent display of majesty. Hitler had no riding skills, and unlike Mussolini never tried to exploit the symbolic value of parading in the saddle. By contrast, Napoleon had a passion for riding, and favoured Arabian horses with their capacity for speed, resilience and manoeuvrability. He also understood the visual impact of the hero and his horse. When Jacques-Louis David was first commissioned to paint his celebrated picture *Napoleon Crossing the Alps* he planned to show the First Consul with an unsheathed sabre in his hand, but Napoleon dictated otherwise: 'No, my dear David, battles are not won by the sword. I wish to be painted sitting calmly on a spirited (*fougueux*) horse.'

Dutton's Maharajah draws its power from the contrast the dignified rider makes with his vivacious mount. Just as she intended, her statue as a whole is animated by the horse's elegant liveliness. With its upraised foreleg, thrashing tail and intelligent head, the creature invests the figure with an appropriate sense of majesty, which in turn is conveyed by the Maharajah's control of his steed. He allows the animal to exercise its natural vitality – it wilfully turns its head – but he calmly maintains control, his poise and command untroubled, while he looks steadfastly towards the east.

Only two pictures of Duleep Singh mounted on a horse are to be found in Peter Bance's book, *Sovereign, Squire & Rebel*; both date from his teenage years in India, and one is of dubious validity.[ccxxx] Likewise, Google's large collection of images of Duleep Singh does not include a single one that shows him on horseback. The truth was that in later life he became too fat to sit comfortably on a horse, and even if he had been fond of riding he would hardly have cut a heroic figure. By the same token, the sword in the statue's left hand referred to the Sikhs' great warrior tradition, but Duleep Singh himself was never given the chance to be a soldier, or even wear a ceremonial military uniform. He was exposed to some horrific bloodshed as a child, but once he became a charge of the British he was kept well away from any military experience.

But all this is beside the point. Dutton's statue is not a portrait of Duleep Singh, it is an evocation of the Maharajah's significance in the eyes of the Sikh community, as envisaged by the Trust: 'The image we wanted to put in the minds of visitors to Butten Island was of a Sikh nobleman.' Duleep Singh had his faults, which were a matter of historical record, but the Trust was determined that they should not be a reason for the Sikhs to disown him. Many of his imperfections and personal failings were the result of his upbringing, and although he proceeded to add a few on his own initiative they had nothing to do with the bronze Maharajah that the Trust wished to raise on Butten Island. The statue was, above all, a symbol of the British Sikhs' self-respect. Ranjit Singh would have made a more genuinely heroic subject, but he was not a British figure; he had not undergone the challenge of an émigré's life. The Duleep Singh on his horse in Thetford was Maharajah of a mythical kingdom where the *khanda* flag flew and Sikh pride was restored. 1999 was the year of another anniversary, one that was not celebrated: it was the 150th anniversary of the Treaty of Lahore in 1849. No other Sikh, however heroic, could be the symbolic ruler of the Sikhs during that century and a half of their experience as exiles from their own sovereignty. Duleep Singh was the British Maharajah of the modern Sikh, a title that was fraught with as many paradoxes as the man himself.

Twelve

CONTEMPLATIVE SPACE

When it came to the design of the memorial site, the Trust was no less fortunate, or astute, in its choice of architect, than it had been in its choice of sculptor.

John Wormald, working from his practice in Edgbaston, produced a design in 1993 for a site close to the road in Elveden, presumably before a decision had finally been made to take the monument elsewhere. It comprised what he called a 'court', or paved square, with an equestrian statue standing on a wedge-shaped plinth as its centrepiece. The court was approached by way of a little bridge over a dry moat that led to an avenue of masonry monoliths with decorative capitals. The southern side was enclosed by a marble veneered wall carrying inscribed texts. Trees and benches round the perimeter provided an air of seclusion and peace.

To accompany the plan, Wormald wrote a brief treatise to explain the purpose of his design, which from its first line showed that he was in harmony with the ambitions of the Trust. 'The intention of the memorial is to ... illustrate the links symbolised between Indian and English, and between Sikh and western cultures.'[ccxxxi] He went on to explain that while the memorial would inform the visitor it would also induce a religious, or at least a meditative mood. It was based 'on the traditional principle of a symbolic routeway', and would present the visitor with 'areas of significance', imitating the way pilgrims are invited to 'walk in a set pattern, visiting shrines along their way, and arriving in a heightened state of awareness at the most important part of their trip.' The route into and out of the court was intended to transport visitors from the everyday, outside world, taking them across a symbolic barrier and delivering them into a contemplative space.

As we have seen, the Elveden site was never accepted, and in due course Wormald was obliged to create a new design suitable for Butten Island. The statue and its paved area were to be located at the western end of the island, close to the bridge that carried people walking from the shopping precinct on the north side.

Many features were different from the earlier design, and several were not ultimately installed, but the basic principles remained the same. As Wormald explained in a second treatise written for his new design, the Thet and the Little Ouse 'would provide a physical barrier to approaching the monument itself, and would also act as a symbolic barrier or division, between the everyday, and the special commemorative, contemplative space which is the memorial.[ccxxxii]

In Wormald's conception the Maharajah on his horse was to be the focus of a topographical plan designed to take pedestrians through a quasi-spiritual experience. Crossing the bridge was to be a transformative moment, as one perceptual world was exchanged for another. An illusory perspective created by the use of columns of steadily increasing height would then draw the visitor into the heart of the memorial.

The idea that crossing a humble pedestrian bridge can be a spiritually transformative experience may seem fanciful at first, yet most people who cross a bridge on foot, whose minds are not unavoidably preoccupied by mundane things, are tempted to pause, if only mentally, and enjoy a moment that must be described as philosophical or, for those so inclined, as religious. Bridges of all sizes, but especially those that carry one across rivers, prompt such moments, no matter how fleeting. To cross a bridge is to liberate yourself from your normal, earthly constraints. Even the most functional structure launches you on an adventure unique to bridges: you defy gravity without being a bird, and if the bridge crosses a river you traverse water without being a fish. Every bridge is at once functional and symbolic: it connects, it separates, and it creates a neutral interim. There is something exhilarating about setting foot on a bridge, launching yourself into space and escaping the world on one side before entering the world on the other. For a moment you hang in suspension, floating above the flow of both time and water, and in that no man's land you are free to let the mind cross bridges of its own.

The bridge in Thetford that crosses the Little Ouse and the Thet where they converge is a three-legged construction, painted a suitably pastoral green. A plaque attached to its railing informs the pedestrian that 'This bridge was provided in October 1968 jointly by Thetford Borough Council and Norwich Union Insurance Group for the benefit of the townspeople of Thetford.' As it happens, three-way or tri-bridges, as they are sometimes called, are a great rarity; indeed, according to Wikipedia there are only forty-one in the world, five of them in the United Kingdom. The definition is strict: a three-way bridge (or tri-bridge) must have three distinct and separate spans, with one end of each span meeting at a common point near the centre of the bridge. This exactly describes the Thetford example.[ccxxxiii] It is additionally unusual in having no central pillar or support at the point where the three spans come together; the weight is sustained in mid-air by the upward thrust of the three parts as they push against each other. All bridges possess an element of daring, but in the case of Thetford's bridge it is intensified by this seemingly miraculous device.[ccxxxiv] Wormald made good use of the opportunity it offered.

As you approach the bridge, with your back to the shopping precinct, you see that the span rises slightly to a peak at the centre, where the three legs combine, and this little elevation promises to lift you above the town, while granting you a coign of vantage to view the two rivers as they merge. Stepping from the riverside promenade onto the bridge, you bid goodbye to shops, streets and offices. The river ripples beneath your feet; swans glide on the water; you are raised by the cant of the bridge above the humdrum world. You have crossed Wormald's 'symbolic barrier'.

At the central point, the bridge divides and presents you with choices. You can turn right towards the new Travelodge hotel, beside which a statue of Captain Mainwaring of Dad's Army fame sits on a bench, dreaming of victory over Mr Hitler. Or you can pause to lean on the rail, stare at the water, and let your mind set sail like a paper boat on the current. Or you can turn left and descend towards Butten Island. By making the last decision you will have opted for the cerebral over the material, for recreation over business, for the aesthetic over the practical. The island has nothing to offer except pleasure; it has no other function. For a few hundred yards you will have the chance to let your mind slip its leash. You will have been delivered into the contemplative space that Wormald visualised.

At the foot of the bridge Wormald had intended the visitor's eye to be drawn towards the statue by an avenue of columns, but it was never built. However, the trees surrounding the statue have matured and these days they provide a leafy setting that serves as both canopy and screen, isolating the statue in a kind of natural temple large enough to accommodate it. (The statue and its plinth together stand nearly fourteen feet high.)

Wormald had also intended that a 'marble-faced slab monolith' would be placed near the path, which would be inscribed with 'introductory and interpretive information', equipping visitors who knew nothing about Duleep Singh to understand what they were about to look at. The monolith was never installed, and as things stand visitors must make what they can of the text on the plinth itself. Finally, Wormald had planned for a set of 'simple stone plaques' to be set around the base of the statue, representing the Maharajah's descendants. They too never materialised.

Wormald did not realign the existing paths on the island, partly out of a desire to make a discreet impact on the topography, but also because the path running beside the river drew visitors towards the statue obliquely, allowing their viewpoint to rotate as they walked.

After a short walk visitors who have followed the path will find themselves on the threshold of a paved area made of stone slabs and flints, which at first sight appears to be in the shape of a keyhole with the statue standing at its centre.

In fact, this shape is derived from the *khanda*, the standard symbol of the Sikh faith, which is stamped in gold on the front face of the plinth with the motto 'Deg Teg Fateh'. This slogan signifies the dual responsibilities carried by Sikhs: to provide food and protection to those in need, *deg* meaning cauldron or kettle and *teg* meaning sword. The kettle symbolises the charitable obligation placed on Sikhs to provide food for everybody, and the sword represents the Sikh warrior code. Both these concepts are contained in the *khanda* icon:

It consists of a double-edged sword, enclosed within a circle, which in turn is enclosed within two curved swords. Each component has its own symbolic significance. The doubled-edged sword in the centre is a metaphor of divine knowledge, whose sharp edges cleave truth from falsehood. The *chakar* surrounding it is the circle without beginning or end that symbolises the perfection of God. The two outer curved swords are called *kirpans*, and they represent the twin concepts of temporal and spiritual authority, and are used to express the equal emphasis that a Sikh must place on spiritual aspirations and obligations to society.[ccxxxv]

The Trust sometimes claims that Duleep Singh's significance is strictly political, and that by the same token so is the significance of his statue, yet the design of the monument makes it clear that the whole site was intended to carry as much religious as political symbolism. But then, as the *khanda* illustrates, the two are inseparable in Sikh doctrine.

Walking down the path towards the statue, the visitor directly confronts the Maharajah and his steed; he is at the heart of Wormald's contemplative space. The architect has done his job, and now the statue must do its own spiritual and aesthetic work.

Thirteen

PRINCE TO PRINCE

On 29 July 1999 the great day dawned when the statue was finally unveiled on top of its plinth in its official site on Butten Island. None other than the Prince of Wales was on hand to perform the ceremony. All the efforts of the Trust had at last reached their triumphant fruition.

In 1998 the Prince had received an invitation from Thetford Borough Council to mark the 800th anniversary of Thetford's mayoralty, a rare distinction. The council was pleased to be able to strengthen its invitation by proposing a busy programme of events, to which they added the unveiling of the Maharajah's statue. The Prince had accepted.

On arriving in Thetford, he was taken to King's House, Thetford's town hall, where a reception was held in his honour and the Mayor introduced him to Denise Dutton,

John Wormald, and members of the Trust. He was then driven to Butten Island and, as *The East Anglian Daily Times* wittily put it, 'the prince met ... the prince.'[tcxxxvi] The sun shone, a respectful crowd gathered around the plinth, and the Prince pulled back orange curtains to reveal its inscription. Above him, his fellow prince rode his horse, majestic and impassive. If representatives of Elveden estate or the Iveagh family were present, it went unreported.

After the ceremony the Prince was presented with a Sikh sword, and he was then taken to perform his last duty of the day, the opening of the Gentle Bridge, a footbridge a few hundred yards upstream.

As far as the records show, the Prince did not make a speech. However, a member of the Trust was reported as saying, 'The importance of this occasion cannot be over-stressed. It is a tremendous day in the history of East Anglia and for the Sikh community. It restores Duleep Singh to his rightful place in history. He was a key figure in the cementing of Anglo-Sikh relations. Prince Charles' presence today is very fitting because the Maharajah was very close to the royals and Queen Victoria in particular. We have waited six years for this and today we remove the veil of anonymity that surrounds him.'[tcxxxvii]

Glossing Duleep Singh's history for its readers, *The East Anglian Daily Times* repeated the usual misinformation about the Koh-i-noor. 'He became a friend of Queen Victoria, who was godmother to several of his children, and gave the Koh-i-Noor diamond, now centrepiece of the Crown Jewels, to Britain.'[tcxxxviii] *The Guardian* repeated the same untruth, but reported Harbinder Singh as saying, 'This historic day restores Duleep Singh to his rightful place in history, not just for the Sikh community but for the British people as well... The fact that Prince Charles has come here today is a fitting tribute to the relationship between the Sikh community and the royal family, which is based on mutual admiration.[cxxxix]

The day appears to have passed off to everyone's satisfaction, though Denise Dutton was disappointed to see that her name was nowhere to be seen on the statue or plinth, an oversight the Trust intends to rectify.

None of the press reports referred to the inscription on the plinth, but there must have been some people among the crowd who wondered about its wording, which in effect Prince Charles had endorsed by his official unveiling. What, for instance, had His Royal Highness made of the final phrase: 'To this day the Sikh nation aspires to regain its sovereignty'? If he thought the wording was contentious when he drew aside the orange curtains, he kept it to himself. It was, after all, too late.

The Trust had deliberately not invited any representatives from the Indian High Commission, but if any Indians were present at the ceremony it would be interesting to know what they thought of the Sikhs' aspiration to recover their sovereignty, and what they thought of the official, royal approval which the Sikhs' aspiration had implicitly received.

In recent years the royal family had shown a warm interest in the Sikh community. For instance, the Queen had visited Amritsar only two years earlier in 1997, against the advice of the Indian Prime Minister. Her tour of India had not been a great success, but in Amritsar she was given 'a rapturous welcome', according to *The Independent*. She laid a wreath at the memorial where hundreds of people had been killed in Jallianwala Bagh park in 1919 by British soldiers under the orders of General Dyer.[ccxl] She also visited the Golden Temple, where by special dispensation she was spared the indignity of having to walk barefoot; instead, she was permitted to change into a fresh pair of socks, and to keep her hat on.

The Prince of Wales and the Duchess of Cornwall visited the Punjab in 2006, during which they visited some farms and paid their respects at the famous Sikh shrine in Anandpur Sahib. On this occasion the royal pair took off their shoes and socks, and knelt side by side with their palms on the floor as they lowered their heads to the floor of the temple, which had been laid with fresh white sheets. Charles' head was tightly bound with a maroon scarf worn like a bandana.[ccxli]

Prince Charles may not have spoken at the unveiling, but he had often expressed his admiration for the Sikhs and acknowledged Britain's debt of gratitude to their soldiers. He had even floated the idea of raising a Sikh regiment within the British Army.[ccxlii] On 24 April 2008 he made a speech at a reception to mark the Sikh Festival of Vaisakhi in St James' Palace in London. He referred to his visit in 2006 to Anandpur, where the Sikh Khalsa had been initiated in 1699, and commended the work of the Trust and its successor, the Anglo Sikh Heritage Trail. He singled Harbinder Singh out for special praise, saying, 'I always enjoy listening to him because I learn a great deal from him about the great history of the Sikhs.[ccxliii]

Another member of the royal family had showed his support for the Trust on an earlier occasion, in September 1997, when the Duke of York (Prince Andrew) gave the address at the annual dinner of the Trust in Wentworth. He opened his remarks by saying that he had been struck by 'the fascinating story of Prince Duleep Singh's life' and 'his closeness to Queen Victoria and Prince Albert'. (The title 'Prince' which was often conferred on Duleep Singh and other exiled Indian rulers, was of course an honorary and British one.) He went on to say that the Maharajah's life was 'an enchanting chapter' in Anglo-Sikh history.

His talk mostly concentrated on the Sikhs' remarkable contribution to the British Army during two world wars, and he finished by saying that he wished to endorse the work of the Trust in promoting an increased awareness of the shared history underpinning Anglo-Sikh relations.[ccxliv]

This was not a state occasion. On the contrary, it was a private event, and it is worth noting that Prince Andrew opened his remarks by recalling the close personal relationship between Queen Victoria and Duleep Singh. One can only speculate, but it may well be that the present royal family continues to feel an affinity with the Sikhs as a result of the 'special' connection between their predecessors, notably Queen Victoria, and the Maharajah and his family, which was based on a private attachment, rather than official requirements. At a personal level this affinity must necessarily be one-sided nowadays, since there are no direct descendants of Duleep Singh, but perhaps the British Sikhs in general are the beneficiaries of the long-standing link.

The American academic Martin Wainwright has suggested that Duleep Singh's attachment to Queen Victoria, which lasted all his life, was based on more than his affection for a mother figure and protector. He wrote that 'Duleep consistently clung to his identity as the maharaja of Punjab, but for him this title had little to do with Indian or Sikh nationalism. Nor did it preclude him from considering himself a subject of Queen Victoria. For Duleep's concept of allegiance was neither ethnic nor national. Rather it was *dynastic*, and it thrived on the personal ties that were possible in an empire that retained the concept of subjecthood to the monarch rather than citizenship of the state.'[ccxlv] (My emphasis.)

According to Wainwright, Duleep Singh adopted a dual identity, which was only feasible under a 'pre-modern' concept of loyalty. As Maharajah he continued to think of himself as the lawful sovereign of Punjab (his own self-description), but he also recognised that his sovereignty had been curtailed by the East India Company's military victory over his army in 1846. 'He therefore regarded himself as a king who owed allegiance to the British monarch. In this sense he also considered himself a British subject', that is a subject of the Queen herself, an identification that Victoria wholeheartedly endorsed.[ccxlvi]

Wainwright pointed out that in Duleep Singh's mind there was a crucial distinction between the government and the monarch, and for the latter his loyalty was unwavering. (His contempt for the former was no less consistent.)

This concept of loyalty as a result of military defeat helps to explain Duleep Singh's willingness to endorse Victoria's ownership of the Koh-i-noor. It belonged to her, not because he thought its looting was justified, but because it was hers by right as the ruler of the Punjab. However, his deference to the victor did not diminish his sense of his own royalty. When the Queen and Gladstone decided in 1873 that Duleep Singh should be offered a peerage, his reply was emphatic: 'I thank Her Majesty. Most heartily and humbly convey to her my esteem and admiration. Beyond that I cannot go. I claim myself to be royal; I am not English, and neither I nor my children will ever become so. Such titles – though kindly offered, we do not heed and cannot assume. We love the English and especially their Monarch, but we must remain Sikhs.'[ccxlvii]

With this concept of 'dynastic' allegiance in mind, an allegiance paid by one royal person to another, it is not far-fetched to speculate that today's British royal family have inherited a particular sense of obligation towards Duleep Singh and by extension to the Sikhs – an obligation owed by one royal dynasty to the memory of another.

The East Anglian Daily Times was not so far off the mark when it talked about the prince meeting the prince.

Fourteen

MAHARAJAH RESTORED

Since that day in July 1999, the bronze Maharajah on his horse has ruled over his island in Thetford. In the end he did recover a kingdom; not the Punjab, not the empire of his father, but at least a part of England, where he is the undisputed sovereign ruler. His remains are buried at Elveden, but he is resurrected on Button Island in a version of his father's glory: mounted on a kingly horse, bearing the sword of his rulership, the great diamond on his arm. His rule is benign, and in a kind of imperial redemption his subjects are now both Asian and British, Sikh and non-Sikh. No one wishes to depose him from his throne in Norfolk, and his honorary subjects among the Sikhs, whom Thetford welcomes, come in large numbers to venerate his memory.[ccxlviii]

All statues are heroic in that they must keep their solitary vigils through all weathers and seasons, day and night, year in, year out. No one comes to relieve them, and they must remain at their posts eternally, or at least as long as their subjects do not fall out of favour with the public. History is no protection and statues must share the reputational fates of their originals. Once they fall from grace, their statues may fall too, toppled into the dust and broken up or melted down. In this respect Duleep Singh can be said to have had the last laugh. After Independence many statues from the colonial era in New Delhi were ignominiously carted off to the Coronation Ground, once the site of the Raj's most spectacular ceremonial displays of imperial power. The fifty-foot statue of George V is reported to be still standing, but a marble bust of Queen Victoria has not fared so well. It was removed to the Coronation Ground, but never lifted onto its designated plinth. In 2007 a reporter found the bust lying face-up in the mud, but in 2011 the same journalist could not find it, and he speculated that the Empress of India had been crushed to make gravel.[ccxlix]

For most of his reign over Butten Island the Maharajah has been treated with respect, but there have been a couple of lapses. On one occasion Thetford woke up to discover that the Maharajah's turban had been painted orange. The insult was probably a drunken prank rather than a hostile act, and the choice of colour was accidentally ironic, since an orange turban signifies wisdom. On another occasion an attempt was made to damage the marble facing of the plinth, but this appears to have been the result of 'exuberant youth' (Harbinder Singh's phrase) rather than racist malice.

The statue has only been seriously vandalised once, and that was in March 2005 when white paint was poured over the Maharajah's figure, in a streak covering its face and chest. Swastikas and the letters NF (National Front) were also spray-painted on the monument, indicating that it was a racially motivated crime. In itself this was curious: while Thetford was a multi-ethnic town, its Asian population was small, and its Sikh population had always been negligible. On behalf of the town, Ray Key, the Mayor of Thetford, was outraged by the vandals who had 'desecrated' Duleep Singh's statue, and he called them 'despicable' and 'sick'. 'I am absolutely livid about this,' he said. 'I can't put it into words. They should be put in prison... [The statue] means a lot to the Sikh nation and we're privileged to have it in our town. It's been a lovely feature in a beautiful area... We are so pleased and proud to have this statue in this town. I am ashamed. It is a slur on the town.'[ccl] Speaking in the same spirit, the police, represented by Inspector Peacock, said that the crime was 'of a racial nature' and the offenders would be prosecuted 'to the full extent of the law'.[ccli] Unfortunately, the offenders were never identified, and no prosecutions took place. Speaking on behalf of the Trust, Harbinder Singh said he was 'very saddened' by the attack, adding that it was 'the act of mindless and cowardly imbeciles. It is insulting the values of all of us.'[cclii] The Trust arranged to have the statue cleaned, at considerable expense, and no trace of the attack remains visible.

From time to time the statue has required other sorts of maintenance. For example, it was discovered recently that the statue was sinking and tipping slightly, and work had to be done on the subterranean platform that supported the whole structure. As a result of the subsidence, the last line of the inscription that refers to the Sikh nation's aspiration to 'regain its sovereignty' almost disappeared beneath the level of the surrounding grass, an effect that was symbolically unfortunate. The repairs made it necessary for the plinth to be enclosed by protective metal fencing in 2015, which provided another unintended and regrettable symbol: the Maharajah appeared to be imprisoned, not in Elveden's gilded cage, but something more like a gaol. As soon as the renovation was completed the fencing was taken down, and the Maharajah was restored to his kingly dignity. Plans are afoot to protect the statue from flooding and to enhance the site with lighting and benches that will allow visitors to enjoy the contemplative space originally envisaged by Wormald.

The expense of maintaining the statue is currently borne by the Anglo Sikh Heritage Trail, a new organisation that was launched in July 2004 and more or less replaced the original Trust. Like the Trust, it was designed to promote greater awareness of the heritage shared by the Sikhs and the British. Today the Trail directs Sikhs to more than forty places and institutions associated with Duleep Singh, some of which are clustered round Thetford: the Ancient House

Museum, the statue on Butten Island, the grave at Elveden, as well as places associated with the Maharajah's second son, Prince Frederick, who lived in the district for most of his life.[ccliii] When the Trust was first formed in 1993, its founders wanted to ensure that Duleep Singh's memory was retrieved from the historical obscurity in which it had fallen. It is fair to say that between them the Trust and the Trail have gone a long way to realising that objective as more and more books, pictures, films, documentaries and tourist sites add to his commemoration.

For nearly a century and a half Winterhalter's portrait of Duleep Singh in his silks and jewels, commissioned by Queen Victoria, was the normative and much imitated image of the Maharajah. Dutton's statue in Thetford, though much more austere, was in the same idealised, romantic tradition, and like Winterhalter's picture called on the spectator to admire its hero. Then, in 2013, a remarkable portrait of Duleep Singh was exhibited that called for a very different response, a political portrait that sought to engage in an argument about the Maharajah. Its very title, *Casualty of War*, threw down the gauntlet.

It was the work of The Singh Twins, contemporary British artists and sisters who paint together.[ccliv] Their portrait was commissioned by the National Museum of Scotland, where it now hangs. It was designed to be a response to pieces of jewellery and other objects in the museum's collection that once belonged to Duleep Singh's elder son, Prince Victor, who had sold large parts of his inheritance at an auction in 1899.

Using poster paint, gouache and gold dust, The Singh Twins painted the picture in their characteristic style, drawing on the eighteenth-century miniaturist tradition of Indian art. It is a complex and dense work with suitably Victorian echoes in its Pre-Raphaelite choice of sharply rendered details, brilliant colours and symbolic floral decoration.

The picture is ingeniously composed to present two, apparently simultaneous time dimensions. At its centre is a highly ornamented arch replicating the plaster arch that Duleep Singh installed in Elveden Hall. This arch encloses a blue sky that forms the background for Duleep Singh's head, but also frames an imaginary topography containing many features of his tragic Punjabi childhood and adolescence: the gateway of the fort in Lahore, the Sutlej River stained with blood, the church and Login's official residence in Fatehgarh, where Duleep Singh was first exiled as a deposed prince. Lying outside the arch is the world of his adulthood, represented by various buildings and places scattered across the green meadows of England, among them Osborne House, Menzies Castle, his town house in Holland Park, as well as two graves, his own and Login's in Felixstowe.

The figure of Duleep Singh straddles these two dimensions: he sits within the arch, but is at work on a desk that obtrudes into the adult sphere. His desk is covered with a Kashmiri shawl and loaded with precious objects that refer to his education at the hands of the British – 'everything required for a young boy to be groomed in the manners, faith and values of Victorian society,' to quote the painters' own commentary on their picture.[cclv]

In their lengthy commentary on the picture The Singh Twins stated that they had modelled their version of the Maharajah on Winterhalter's portrait, partly because it was painted the year he arrived in Britain and therefore marks the beginning of his story as Britain's first resident Sikh. In fact, their portrait shows an older Duleep Singh, fuller in the face and sporting a mature beard, but it does reproduce the opulence of Winterhalter's work. Their Maharajah is loaded with jewels – rubies, emeralds, sapphires, pearls, diamonds. 'This,' the Twins declare, 'is the young Sikh Maharajah in all his splendour, imagined by the artists as he would and should have been, had his rightful position as Sikh Emperor of Punjab not been taken from him.[cclvi]

For The Singh Twins the jewels serve as the ultimate symbol of Duleep Singh's status: what he was when he inherited his throne, and what he lost when he was deposed. They were symbols of both power and surrender, of conquest and theft at the hands of British imperialism. While studying the Museum's jewels, the artists felt a special connection with the Maharajah. 'Handling them was very sad for us. And exciting… But there's anger and resentment too. Why are these things here? They tell the story of a man who surrounded himself with objects that somehow still encapsulated his identity.[cclvii]

The items in the picture are as carefully arranged as a display in a jeweller's display case, with the green and blue backgrounds serving as a kind of velvet. The little vignettes – one might almost call them pictograms – that make up the intricate design of the picture are all deployed to advance the argument that emerges from the whole work. The Twins intended their portrait to be both a likeness and a biographical narrative, but their picture might be better described as an indictment. It amounts to a charge sheet of the many injustices done to Duleep Singh, for every detail refers to some cruelty or humiliation inflicted on him by the British; hence its title *Casualty of War*.

To take one especially concentrated area, we see that the Maharajah wears three amulets on his left arm, including the Koh-i-noor diamond set between two teardrop diamonds. Beside it, and leading out of the Punjabi archway onto the green grass of English exile, is a drawing based on an illustration which appeared in *The Pictorial Times* that shows Duleep Singh on an elephant as he rode for the last time in his pomp to surrender to the British. This doomed procession leads the eye directly to the Maharajah's grave in Elveden, to which has been added the Sikh *khanda* symbol. A tendril bearing a raspberry fruit connects the tomb to the famous Spy cartoon, published in *Vanity Fair*, of Duleep Singh in middle age – fat, debauched and smoking a cigar. 'This representation of Duleep Singh,' The Singh Twins wrote in their commentary, 'as the "tamed", "English, Christian, gentleman" is a sad reminder of what he was reduced to under British manipulation and rule.[cclviii]

The tone of the picture is set by the flowers that twine in a daisy chain round the edge of the composition, another motif that draws on Victorian and Indian traditions. Every plant makes a symbolic contribution to the polemic: the Punjabi paisley motif imprinted with an English rose represents British domination of the Punjab, which was built on avarice (alpine auricula), lust for wealth (orchid) and deceit (thorn apple). Various emotions associated with Duleep Singh are also represented: remorse (raspberries), stubborn pride (thistle) and injustice (hop flower). A wreath of hemlock, marigolds and monkshood placed on Duleep Singh's grave represents 'death, deceit and ill luck; pain and grief; and crime, treachery and the poison of words, respectively.[cclix]

In an interview for *The Guardian* in 2014, The Singh Twins said that Duleep Singh's 'life was filled with longing for his homeland, no matter how English and Christian he became. As British-born Sikhs, we can identify with that sense of loss, that pining for a heritage, that identity confusion.[cclx] Their picture was a kind of riposte to the Winterhalter portrait, because it 'reimagines the Maharaja as he was never permitted to be: as ruler of his kingdom, in traditional finery, surrounded by objects that were surrendered to the British.' It showed him 'as the Maharaja was supposed to be.[cclxi]

Summing up their feelings about the Maharajah, The Singh Twins said, 'His life was so complex. He always had people telling him what to do, who to be. He was moulded into a Christian gentleman, then would be asked to wear full Indian dress when paraded at Victoria and Albert's parties. There was that sense that he would never truly be one of them, which British Asians can still identify with. But he also had a great affection for Britain, the Logins and Victoria… There is no way of reconciling this man's identity.[cclxii]

In conversation with me, The Singh Twins explained that for them Duleep Singh was a symbol of the Sikhs' lost heritage. They said that all young British Sikhs should know about him, because he represented a part of who they were, both ancestrally and culturally. Knowing Duleep Singh's story would enable them to find their own place within modern society. Duleep Singh was a role model in that he possessed a fighting spirit, which led him to fight against the injustices done to him. Part of the Sikh heritage was to stand up and speak out against injustice. It was always important to look back to your roots in order to understand your identity. They said that their painting was about the Anglo-British connection; it was concerned with empire and colonialism, issues that were with us today, and still symbolised by the Koh-i-noor. History leaves its imprint on debates about contemporary culture. Their painting was not just about loss, but the consequences of migration, and how, in the case of the Sikhs, immigrants had contributed to the fabric of British life. In this way the story of Duleep Singh was relevant to both Sikhs and non-Sikhs.[cclxiii]

Casualty of War is an angry picture, and in that respect it differs in spirit from the statue in Thetford, which exudes an air of detached serenity. It might be argued, as The Singh Twins do, that because the statue in Thetford bears no resemblance to its subject and depicts him in a plain, ahistorical costume, it separates the Maharajah from his historical context, and therefore reduces his significance. However, both works depict a man who never was. The Singh Twins have painted an authentic likeness, but by their own admission they have also created a portrait that shows the Maharajah 'as he should have been'. The Thetford statue has a similar ambition, but uses different means. True, the figure is lifted out of history, but Dutton's statue has made use of an ancient iconography that is less concerned with likeness and context, and more concerned with conveying a sense of power and majesty. This quality also has its part to play in the establishment of British Sikh identity.

The inscription on the plinth below the statue strikes a different note. We recall that its last line states, 'To this day the Sikh nation aspires to regain its sovereignty.' And this follows the lines that tell the spectator that Duleep Singh died in Paris, 'having re-embraced the Sikh faith and whilst still engaged in a struggle to reclaim his throne.' Remembering the tumultuous events that overtook Punjab for nearly a decade following Operation Blue Star in 1984, how are we to interpret the text on the plinth?

According to Singh and Tatla, Duleep Singh has become an icon for the new generation of British Sikhs, a tangible link with royalty for 're-imagining' the British Sikh experience. 'As the British Sikh community seeks to establish a new identity, one which transcends the familiar image of racialised migrants, Duleep Singh's legacy provides an enduring symbol of Sikhs' British attachment as well as the potential for dissonance and ultimate rebellion.[cclxiv] Was this what the Trust had in mind: dissonance and rebellion?

Harbinder Singh was largely responsible for drafting the text on behalf of the Trust in 1993, and he elucidated its wording for me.[cclxv] 'Operation Blue Star,' he said, 'told the Sikhs yet again that we were not masters of our own fate.'

Control of our destiny had been taken out of our hands in 1849 and then again, a century later, in 1947. After the debacle of 1984 we needed to look back on our history and find something to feel good about. In these circumstances, Duleep Singh took on a fresh importance. He was our last sovereign. He was a poignant reminder that we had once possessed our own sovereign kingdom. Above all, he was a figure that symbolised an era when we had been powerful and independent – an era we could look back on with pride. Duleep Singh also represented a bond connecting Britain and the homeland of Punjab. He was the first Sikh settler, and he served to remind Sikhs that their relationship with the British had not always been subservient. We had signed a treaty of friendship as equals.

In 1993 we were very conscious of the injustices we felt the Sikhs had suffered during the decade that had followed Operation Blue Star. Sovereignty at that time was a burning issue, but by using the word on the plinth we did not mean to imply separatism or secession. For the Trust the term sovereignty referred to the status the Sikhs had enjoyed when the Punjab was our homeland before the British had intervened. The sovereignty we 'aspired' to was essentially symbolic. The phrase was a way of consoling ourselves with the idea that the Sikhs had once had a kingdom, to which we could return as a source of self-respect. We were sure that the Prince of Wales had understood the words in that spirit.

The wounds inflicted by the Indian government in 1984 were still raw, and for that reason the Trust deliberately did not invite anyone from the Indian High Commission in 1999. The statue and its unveiling by the Prince of Wales was a British affair, a celebration for British Sikhs, and had nothing to do with the Indians. We were British subjects remembering our mutual history. The event was a declaration of loyalty to Britain, and a retelling of the narrative that bound the British and the Sikhs together. We would not have been standing together in Thetford on 29 July 1999 if the East India Company had not annexed Punjab in 1849.

As for saying that the Koh-i-noor diamond 'passed' to the British authorities, when in fact it had been forcibly surrendered, we did not want to politicise, or make an issue of its British possession. On the contrary, as long as the diamond was secured in the Tower of London, on exhibition for all to see, it would serve as a reminder to future generations of the Sikhs' heritage. In the future the direct link with the Punjabi homeland will weaken as fewer Sikhs emigrate, and it will be important that the relics of Sikh history are properly cared for and protected. If the Koh-i-noor and other Sikh treasures had been kept in the Golden Temple they might have been destroyed or stolen in 1984.

In one respect Dutton's statue has been assimilated to a heritage unavailable to The Singh Twins' portrait, and that is Thetford's heritage. Even Thetford's most loyal partisan could not claim that the town possesses a rich cultural legacy. Those responsible for tourism must struggle nobly on its behalf since they have precious few resources to work with, but they do have one gilt-edged asset, and that is the town's association with Duleep Singh. He may have been exiled from Elveden, but he has been granted hospitable asylum in Thetford, where he is now promoted as one its local heroes.

Kushwant Singh, the great Sikh writer and historian, once expressed the hope that the day would come when a British Sikh could say with pride, 'I'm a Sikh; I am an Englishman.'[tclxvi] The day he hoped for was surely brought a little closer when the statue of Duleep Singh was unveiled on Butten Island.

Fifteen

A SUNNY DAY IN OCTOBER

It is a sunny afternoon and I am in the churchyard of St Andrew and St Patrick's Church in Elveden. The date is 22 October.

Twenty people or so are gathered round the graves of Duleep Singh, his wife and son. They include the Mayor, who wears his chain of office, several Sikhs (the men distinguishable by their beards and blue turbans), a member of the museum's staff, a representative of the local press, and others, like me, who have come from the Thetford area to pay their respects to the Maharajah.

The graves have recently been restored and in the October sunlight their white marble headstones make a luminous contrast with the sombre flints of the church walls.

On behalf of the Sikhs, Harbinder Singh makes a speech, in which he tells us that 22 October was the day in 1893 when the dreams of the Sikh nation came to an end. He describes the pathetic circumstances of the Maharajah's dying alone in Paris, separated from his people and his faith. Since then, however, the two great kingdoms of the Sikhs and the British have been united. The Sikhs have been loyal to the British crown, serving as soldiers in the First World War. Finally, he says that the Sikh community is grateful to Thetford for the hospitality the town has shown them. The link between the Sikhs and Thetford is very important.

The Mayor responds, saying he has both an official and a personal reason for being proud to place a wreath on the Maharajah's grave. His great-great-grandfather had been Duleep Singh's gamekeeper and had carried his coffin. He too is buried in the churchyard, and he points to the grave, which lies nearby. The Mayor places his wreath on the grave, and is followed by several other men and women who leave posies of flowers.

Once the ceremony is over the group disperses and makes its way back to Thetford where tea will be served in the Bell Hotel.

I will join them, but first I want to revisit the statue on Butten Island, as I have done countless times while writing this book.

As usual, I am not alone: the statue is being photographed from every angle by a Sikh using a professional lens. I do not disturb him. Instead, I walk to one of the benches near the river's edge to think about questions that have concerned me throughout my acquaintance with the statue.

For example, by making a romanticised hero of the Maharajah, has the Trust inadvertently strengthened the umbilical cord that ties the British Sikh community to its colonial past? After all, in order to make a hero out of Duleep Singh, it is necessary to forget that he also signifies the conquest of the Punjab, and hence the demise, not the glory of his father's kingdom. Is a nineteenth-century figure who was broken on the imperial wheel, the kind of hero who is going to restore the Sikhs' self-respect?

I look back at Dutton's prince on his horse and, much as I admire it as a piece of sculpture, I can't help thinking that as political symbolism it has an old-fashioned feel about it. The piece could almost have been sculpted in the Maharajah's own lifetime. Furthermore, it draws on the oldest iconography of all, veneration of a legendary king. But royalism is surely a nostalgic, if not reactionary ideal? Rather than looking forward to a progressive future, the statue harks back to an irretrievable past, which is not a healthy place to rebuild one's pride. Is the prestige of Duleep Singh and his father's great kingdom enough to help young Sikhs construct a modern identity for themselves, one that frees them from the troubled, humiliating past which has tormented their parents and grandparents?

These are questions that cannot be settled. The statue is as full of contradictions as its subject, who in turn bequeathed them to his fellow Sikhs.

I stand up and return to the statue. The photographer has gone and I am alone with the Maharajah. What I do know for certain is that between them the Trust, Denise Dutton and Thetford have given the Sikhs and the town and anyone else who cares to walk on Butten Island a fine monument to a man who should not be forgotten. I am moved when I remember that the Sikhs chose not to 'disown' Duleep Singh, despite his imperfections. They have embraced a legacy that might have been poisonous had they not redeemed it with their loyalty. And Thetford, in its turn, has been loyal to the Sikhs and their quest for a memorial.

I take the path at the end of the paved *khanda*, and walk towards the three-legged bridge. The last of the day's sunshine is glinting on the bronze horseman. He will be there tomorrow.

Appendix I

DULEEP SINGH'S BIOGRAPHERS

The pioneering work was done by Michael Alexander and Sushila Anand in their book *Queen Victoria's Maharajah: Duleep Singh 1838-93*, published in 1979, which quoted extensively from documents held in the Royal Archives at Windsor, the India Office Library and Duleep Singh's correspondence. The complex and often absurd tale of the Maharajah's attempts to play a part in the Great Game by inveigling the Tsar of Russia to support his ill-fated reclamation of Punjab has been forensically untangled by Christy Campbell in *The Maharajah's Box: An Imperial Story of Conspiracy, Love and a Guru's Prophecy* (2000). Peter Bance has devoted himself for many years to collecting memorabilia relating to the Maharajah and his family, and his collection now includes a remarkable gallery of photographs, many of which are displayed in his sumptuous book, *Sovereign, Squire & Rebel: Maharajah Duleep Singh* (2009). The statue's inscription does not mention Duleep Singh's eight children, nor his two wives, but their stories have been told in a book by Anita Anand, which is principally devoted to his remarkable youngest daughter: *Sophia: Princess, Suffragette, Revolutionary* (Bloomsbury, 2015). Finally, every student of Duleep Singh is bound to turn to the memoirs of Lady Login, the wife of Sir John Login, who was put in charge of Duleep Singh's upbringing and education after he was deposed. All accounts of the Maharajah's childhood, adolescence and first years in England rely almost entirely on her two books of memoirs, *Sir John Login and Duleep Singh* (1889) and *Lady Login's Recollections: Court Life and Camp Life 1820-1904* (Smith, Elder & Co, 1916). Fortunately, both these books are readily available in editions reprinted from the original settings by Nirmal Publishers of New Delhi.

Appendix II

THE SINGH TWINS' COAT OF ARMS

The following is a note by The Singh Twins on their design of the coat of arms, which appears on the title page of this book and is also displayed on both sides of statue's plinth immediately above the inscriptions in English and Punjabi:

In 1993, the Maharajah Duleep Singh Centenary Trust commissioned us to design a coat of arms to mark the centenary year of Duleep Singh's death. Our design was based on the coat of arms commissioned by Prince Albert for Duleep Singh. Prince Albert also composed the patronising motto that went with it: *Prodesse quam conspicii* (Do good rather than be conspicuous). A copy carved in wood of this coat arms can be seen in the Ancient House Museum in Thetford.

First and foremost, our interpretation was intended to represent Duleep Singh's Sikh heritage and royal status. The former is symbolised by the *khanda*, emblem of the Sikh religion, the long crossed swords, which denote *miri* and *piri*, or the dual importance of secular and spiritual responsibilities within Sikh teaching, and the colours of saffron and blue, which are associated with the Sikh khalsa. Duleep Singh's royal ancestry and status are symbolised by the falcon, the bird traditionally used in Indian art to denote royalty and nobility. We retained the British lions and coronet of Prince Albert's original design so that our new coat of arms would acknowledge Duleep Singh's dual Anglo-Sikh heritage, something that shaped his life and left its impact on British life through the social and cultural legacies left by him and his English-born children.

THOMAS PAINE AND INDIA

Duleep Singh's statue is a member of an honourable trio in Thetford. In King Street, Thetford's main street, there is a gilded statue of Thomas Paine by Charles Wheeler, unveiled in 1964, and seated on a bench at the north end of Butten Island is the statue of Captain Mainwaring by Sean Hedges-Quinn, unveiled in 2010.

One can only guess what Captain Mainwaring thinks of Duleep Singh as he stares unsmilingly, upright on his humble bench, towards his princely colleague on his horse. Thomas Paine's views are easier to conjecture. As an uncompromising republican, who had nothing but contempt for inherited titles and privilege, Paine would not have viewed Duleep Singh's personal plight with the slightest sympathy. On the other hand, Paine was a defiant anti-imperialist, and Duleep Singh would have wholeheartedly agreed with his denunciation of the East India Company and Robert Clive, whose first plundering expedition to India had made him a multi-millionaire. Writing in *The Pennsylvania Magazine* in 1775, Paine described how Clive, 'not satisfied with uncountable thousands' and 'resolved on accumulating an unbounded fortune', was received in India on his second expedition: 'The wailing widow, the crying orphan, and the childless parent remember and lament; the rival Nabobs court his favour; the rich dread his power, and the poor his severity. Fear and terror march like pioneers before his camp, murder and rapine accompany it, famine and wretchedness follow in the rear.'[cclxvii]

Paine was too preoccupied with events in America to write much about India, but in a short essay entitled 'A Serious Thought', also published in *The Pennsylvania Magazine* in 1775, he made his opinions perfectly clear: 'When I reflect on the horrid cruelties exercised by Britain in the East Indies—How thousands perished by artificial famine—How religion and every manly principle of honour and honesty were sacrificed to luxury and pride—When I read of the wretched natives being blown away, for no other crime than because, sickened with the miserable scene, they refused to fight—When I reflect on these and a thousand instances of similar barbarity, I firmly believe that the Almighty, in compassion to mankind, will curtail the power of Britain.'[cclxviii]

In the same essay Paine expressed the wish that when America achieved its independence it would 'put a stop to the importation of Negroes for sale, soften the hard fate of those already here, and in time procure their freedom.[tclxix]

ACKNOWLEDGEMENTS

I am grateful to the following people:

Harbinder Singh encouraged me from the start, answered my many questions, and sat down with me for two long conversations;

Denise Dutton, the statue's sculptor, spoke to me about her work at length, and I could not have written my chapter about the sculpting of the statue without her help;

Peter Bance was also encouraging and kindly read my final text;

Oliver Bone, Curator of the Ancient House Museum in Thetford talked to me about the statue and read the text, making helpful comments;

Jan Michael looked over the text with her copy editor's sharp eye;

Anthea Durose talked to me about painting her portrait of Duleep Singh;

Amarpal Singh read the historical sections and gave me sound advice;

The Rev. Paul Ensor talked to me about his experience as vicar of Elveden's St Andrew and St Patrick in 1993;

Sheila Childerhouse and Stephen Davey talked about their memories of the statue's coming to Thetford;

As always, my old friend Alvin Handelman gave my text a rigorous inspection and made invaluable suggestions;

My son Jack read the text and on his recommendation I completely recast the second part;

The Singh Twins kindly allowed me to use their decorative motifs as chapter headings, and to use the coat of arms they designed for the Maharajah Duleep Singh Centenary Trust as part of the title page; they also spared me the time during a busy period in their lives to talk to me about Duleep Singh;

Ashley and Wilf Dell generously supported me in the memory of their mother and my friend, Harriet Dell;

The Arts Council gave me a research grant in 2014, which made it possible for me to work on this book;

James Ferguson has been a congenial and sympathetic publisher;

My wife Sally has hospitably entertained Duleep Singh in our house for the last two years, and I thank her for that and much else besides.

ENDNOTES

Two: The Dispossession of Duleep Singh

i https://www.citypopulation.de/php/uk-england-eastofengland.php?cityid=E34004143

ii Gurharpal Singh and Darsham Singh Tatla, *Sikhs in Britain: The Making of a Community* (London: Zed Books, 2006), p. 133.

iii http://www.sikhiwiki.org/index.php/Mandla_v_Dowell_Lee.

iv Anita Anand, *Sophia: Princess, Suffragette, Revolutionary* (London: Bloomsbury, 2015), p. 8.

v https://en.wikipedia.org/wiki/Sikhism#Justice_and_equality

vi Patwant Singh, *The Sikhs* (London: John Murray, 1999), p. 57.

vii Ibid., p. 56.

viii Quoted in Patwant Singh and Jyoti M. Rai, *Empire of the Sikhs: The Life and Times of Maharaja Ranjit Singh* (London: Peter Owen, 2013), p. 49.

ix Ibid., p. 51.

x Quoted in Kushwant Singh, *Ranjit Singh* (London: Penguin,

2001), p. 40.

xi Ibid., p. 50.

xii Anand, *Sophia*, p. 11.

xiii Emily Eden, *Up the Country: Letters from India* (London: Curzon Press, 1978; 1st edition 1844), p. 227.

xiv J. A. Norris, *The First Afghan War 1838-1842* (Cambridge: Cambridge University Press, 1967), p. 239.

xv http://www.sikhiwiki.org/index.php/Maharaja_Ranjit_Singh

xvi William Dalrymple, *Return of a King* (London: Bloomsbury, 2103), p. 59.

xvii Ibid., p. 59.

xviii Brian Keith Axel, *The Nation's Tortured Body* (Durham, NC: Duke University Press, 2001), p. 58 & 59.

xix The Hon. W.F. Osborne, *The Court and Camp of Runjeet Singh* (London: Henry Colburn Publisher, 1840), pp. 72, 73 & 78. Also at https://archive.org/details/courtcampofrunje00osboiala

xx Singh, *Ranjit Singh*, pp. 300-301, footnote 35.

xxi Singh and Rai, *Empire of the Sikhs: The Life and Times of Maharaja Ranjit Singh*, p. 158.

xxii Ibid., p. 161.

xxiii Anand, *Sophia*, p. 14.

xxiv Account taken from Michael Alexander and Sushila Anand, *Queen Victoria's Maharajah: Duleep Singh 1838-93* (New Delhi, Vikas Publishing House PVT Ltd, 1979), p. 4.

xxv https://en.wikipedia.org/wiki/Battle_of_Sobraon

xxvi Anand, *Sophia*, p. 20.

xxvii Peter Bance, *Sovereign, Squire & Rebel: Maharajah Duleep Singh* (London: Coronet House, 2009), p. 23.

xxviii Quoted in Anand, *Sophia*, p. 21.

xxix https://en.wikipedia.org/wiki/Battle_of_Chillianwala

xxx 'First immigrant' is an honorary title, because there may well have been Sikh lascars or sailors serving on British ships and coming ashore in Britain as long ago as the 17th century.

xxxi Lady Login, *Sir John Login and Duleep Singh* (London: W. H. Allen & Co., 1890), p. 136.

Three: Surrender Completed

xxxii Alexander and Anand, *Queen Victoria's Maharajah*, p. 12.

xxxiii Ibid., p. 13.

xxxiv Lady Login, *Sir John Login and Duleep Singh* (London: W. H. Allen, 1890).

xxxv E. Dalhousie Login, *Lady Login's Recollections: Court Life and Camp Life, 1820 – 1904* (London: Smith, Elder & Co., 1916).

xxxvi Lady Login, *Sir John Login and Duleep Singh*, p. 157.

xxxvii Ibid., p. 230.

xxxviii Ibid., p. 232.

xxxix Ibid., p. 257.

xl Ibid., p. 239.

xli Ibid., p. 239.

xlii Ibid., pp. 278.

xliii Alexander and Anand, *Queen Victoria's Maharajah*, p. 30.

xliv Login, *Sir John Login and Duleep Singh*, p. 273.

xlv Alexander and Anand, *Queen Victoria's Maharajah*, p. 37.

xlvi Duleep Singh, *The Maharajah Duleep Singh and the Government: A Narrative* (Lahore: Sang-E-Meel Publications, 1999), p. 113.

xlvii Login, *Sir John Login and Duleep Singh*, pp. 239/240.

xlviii Ibid., p. 330.

xlix Ibid., p. 333.

l Alexander and Anand, *Queen Victoria's Maharajah*, p. 41.

li Login, *Sir John Login and Duleep Singh*, p. 335.

lii Ibid., p. 336.

liii Quoted in Christy Campbell, *The Maharajah's Box* (London: HarperCollins, 2000), p. 61.

liv Dalhousie Login, *Lady Login's Recollections*, p. 114.

lv Quoted in Campbell, *The Maharajah's Box*, p. 63.

lvi Bance, *Sovereign, Squire and Rebel*, p. 177.

lvii Alexander and Anand, *Queen Victoria's Maharajah*, p. 45.

lviii https://www.royalcollection.org.uk/collection/403843/the-maharaja-duleep-singh-1838-93

lix Dalhousie Login, *Lady Login's Recollections*, p. 123.

lx Ibid., p. 123.

lxi See U. Krishnan, *Indian Jewellery: Dance of the Peacock* (Mumbai: India Book House, 2001), pp. 217-221.

lxii Axel, *The Nation's Tortured Body*, p. 55.

lxiii Ibid., p. 55.

lxiv Ibid., p. 54.

lxv Ibid., p. 54.

lxvi Alexander and Anand, *Queen Victoria's Maharajah*, p. 46.

lxvii Peter Bance tells us that the picture did not reach Osborne House, its present home, until November 1912, and it now hangs in the Durbar Corridor. See Bance, *Sovereign, Squire and Rebel*, p. 177.

Four: Koh-i-noor

lxviii Dalhousie Login, *Lady Login's Recollections*, p. 123.

lxix Ibid., p. 123.

lxx Ibid., p. 123.

lxxi The bibliography of books devoted to the Koh-i-noor is considerable, but the most recent, readable and reliable account is William Dalrymple & Anita Anand, *Kohinoor: The Story of the World's Most Infamous Diamond* (New Delhi: Juggernaut Books, 2016).

lxxii Iradj Amini, *Koh-i-noor* (New Delhi: Roli Books, 1994), p. 27.

lxxiii A detailed description of this incident can be found in William Dalrymple, *Return of a King* (London: Bloomsbury, 2013), pp. 31-33. More details are provided in Dalrymple & Anand, *Kohinoor*, pp. 78-80.

lxxiv Singh and Rai, *Empire of the Sikhs*, p. 113.

lxxv Dalrymple & Anand, *Kohinoor*, p. 81.

lxxvi P. N. Chopra (ed.), et al., *A Comprehensive History of Modern India, Volume 3* (New Delhi: Sterling Publishers Private Ltd, 2003), p. 71.

lxxvii Quoted in https://en.wikipedia.org/wiki/Koh-i-Noor.

lxxviii Amini, *The Koh-i-Noor Diamond*, p. 232.

lxxix Dalrymple & Anand, *Kohinoor*, p. 159.

lxxx Details from ibid. p. 166.

lxxxi Dalhousie Login, *Lady Login's Recollections*, p. 124.

lxxxii E. Dalhousie Login, *Lady Login's Recollections*, p. 126.

lxxxiii Alexander and Anand, *Queen Victoria's Maharajah*, p. 48.

lxxxiv Duleep Singh, *The Maharajah Duleep Singh and the Government: A Narrative* (Lahore: Sange-e- Meel publications, 1999), p. 157.

lxxxv Duleep Singh, T*he Maharajah Duleep Singh and the Government*, p. 135.

lxxxvi Alexander and Anand, *Queen Victoria's Maharajah*, p. 43.

lxxxvii Tiffany Jenkins, *Keeping Their Marbles* (Oxford: Oxford University Press, 2016), p. 129.

lxxxviii A shameful footnote:'In 1970 the UNESCO Convention on the Means of Prohibiting and Preventing the Illicit Import, Export and Transfer of Ownership of Cultural Property was adopted by a large number of countries. Its aim was discourage the international trade in stolen antiquities, and it was chiefly directed at institutions and individual collectors. The list of 'cultural property' covered by the Convention, which has 15 categories, among them postage stamps, does not include jewellery. The UK has ratified neither of these instruments, though John Whittingdale, culture secretary, has committed the government to ratifying the former, shamed or shocked into doing so by the wanton destruction of antiquities in Syria and Iraq.' See Jenkins, *Keeping Their Marbles*, p. 151.

lxxxix Shashi Tharour, *Inglorious Empire: What the British Did to India* (London: C. Hurts & Co., 2017), p. 2.

Five: Most Loyal Subject

xc Major G. Carmichael Smith (ed.), *History of the Reigning Family of Lahore* (Calcutta: W. Thacker and Co., 1847) See: https://ia801602.us.archive.org/23/items/historyofreignin00smyt/historyofreignin00smyt.pdf

xci Login, *Sir John Login and Duleep Singh*, p. 346.

xcii Anand, *Sophia*, p. 30.
xciii Login, *Sir John Login and Duleep Singh*, p. 367.
xciv Ibid., p. 378.
xcv Ibid., p. 548.
xcvi Ibid., p. 444.
xcvii Ibid., p. 450.
xcviii Ibid., p. 463.
xcix Ibid., p. 472.
c Ibid., p. 477.
ci Ibid., p. 480.
cii Ibid., p. 480.
ciii Rena L. Hogg, *A Master-Builder on the Nile* (Pittsburgh: United Presbyterian Board of Publication, 1914), p. 117.
civ Ibid., p. 115.
cv Ibid., p. 115.
cvi Ibid., p. 113.
cvii Ibid., p. 115.
cviii Login, *Sir John Login and Duleep Singh*, p. 487.
cix Alexander and Anand, *Queen Victoria's Maharajah*, p. 106.
cx Ibid., p. 113.
cxi Lady Login, *Sir John Login and Duleep Singh*, p. 491.
cxii Bamba gave birth to a son on 4 August 1865, but he died within twenty-four hours, and was never named. He is buried in Kenmore, Perthshire.
cxiii Bance, *Sovereign, Squire & Rebel*, p. 68.
cxiv Ibid. p. 75.
cxv Ibid., p. 76.
cxvi Alexander and Anand, *Queen Victoria's Maharajah*, p. 116.
cxvii Bance, *Sovereign, Squire & Rebel*, p. 77.
cxviii Alexander and Anand, *Queen Victoria's Maharajah*, p. 82.
cxix Bance, *Sovereign, Squire & Rebel*, p. 80.
cxx Alexander and Anand, *Queen Victoria's Maharajah*, p. 171.
cxxi Ibid., p. 173.
cxxii Ibid., p. 174.

cxxiii Ibid., p. 178.

cxxiv Bance, *Sovereign, Squire & Rebel*, p. 82.

cxxv Ibid., p. 83.

cxxvi Campbell, *The Maharajah's Box*, p. 133.

cxxvii Ibid., p. 133.

cxxviii Ada Douglas Weatherill was born on 15 January 1869, according to Bance, *Sovereign, Squire & Rebel*, p. 95.

cxxix Ibid., p. 88.

cxxx Ibid., p. 86.

cxxxi Ibid., p. 87.

cxxxii Campbell, *The Maharajah's Box*, pp. 237-241.

cxxxiii Ibid., pp. 237-241.

cxxxiv Ibid., p 336.

cxxxv Alexander and Anand, *Queen Victoria's Maharajah*, p. 293.

cxxxvi Ibid., p. 293.

Six: Khalistan

cxxxvii Kushwant Singh, *A History of the Sikhs, Volume 2: 1839-2004* (New Delhi: Oxford University Press, 2016), p. 160.

cxxxviii Ibid., p. 164.

cxxxix Jon Wilson, *India Conquered* (London: Simon & Schuster, 2016), p.394.

cxl Singh, *A History of the Sikhs, Volume 2: 1839-2004*, p. 251.

cxli Mark Tully and Satish Jacob, *Amritsar: Mrs Gandhi's Last Battle* (New Delhi: Rupa, 1985), p. 35.

cxlii https://en.wikipedia.org/wiki/Partition_of_India#Punjab

cxliii https://en.wikipedia.org/wiki/Anandpur_Resolution

cxliv http://www.sikhs.nl/downloads/English/Anandpur_Sahib_Resolution.pdf

cxlv http://www.sikhs.nl/downloads/English/Anandpur_Sahib_Resolution.pdf

cxlvi Tully and Jacob, *Amritsar*, p. 35.

cxlvii https://en.wikipedia.org/wiki/Operation_Blue_Star

cxlviii Singh, *A History of the Sikhs, Volume 2: 1839-2004*, p. 362.

cxlix Ibid., p. 376.

cl https://en.wikipedia.org/wiki/1984_anti-Sikh_riots

cli https://www.hrw.org/reports/2007/india1007/3.htm

clii https://www.hrw.org/reports/2007/india1007/3.htm

cliii https://www.hrw.org/reports/2007/india1007/3.htm
Human Rights Violations in Punjab, 10 January 1990.

cliv https://www.amnesty.org/download/Documents/196000/
asa200111991ar.

clv Gurharpal Singh and Darshan Singh Tatla, *Sikhs in Britain:
The Making of a Community* (London: Zed Books, 2006), p. 24.

clvi Singh, *A History of the Sikhs, Volume 2: 1839-2004*, p. 404.

clvii Kushwant Singh, *A History of the Sikhs, Volume 2: 1839-2004*,
p. 432.

clviii Singh and Tatla, *Sikhs in Britain*, p. 124.

Seven: 'Turbaned Invasion'

clix Duleep Singh archive, Ancient House Museum, Thetford.

clx Ibid.

clxi Ibid.

clxii Ibid.

clxiii Ibid.

clxiv Ibid.

clxv Ibid.

clxvi Ibid. Cutting from *Indian Express*, 23 January 1993.

clxvii 'Vicar mediates over Punjabi maharajah statue argy-bhaji',
The Guardian, 20 January 1993.

clxviii Much of what follows derives from Clive Aslet, 'Elveden
Hall', Christie, Manson & Woods Ltd, 1984.

clxix https://en.wikipedia.org/wiki/John_Norton_(architect)

clxx Bance, *Sovereign, Squire & Rebel: Maharajah Duleep Singh*, p.
63.

clxxi Nikolaus Pevsner, *The Buildings of England: Suffolk*
(Harmondsworth: Penguin Books, 1974), p. 199.

clxxii Bance, *Sovereign, Squire & Rebel*, pp. 69 and 72.

clxxiii Campbell, *The Maharajah's Box*, p. 97.

clxxiv Ibid., p. 428.

clxxv I am grateful to Harbinder Singh for pointing this out to me.

clxxvi This seems hardly credible, but Aslet's undocumented assertion is to be found in *The Edwardian Country House* (Frances Lincoln Limited, 2012), p. 69. He refers to the town as 'Burnham', but he must surely mean Burnham Market, which had a railway station, rather than Burnham on Sea or Burnham on Crouch.

clxxvii https://historicengland.org.uk/listing/the-list/list-entry/1037611

clxxviii Dominic Bradbury, 'Lord and Lady Iveagh – Elveden', *House and Garden, House and Garden*, 2011 – see, http://www.dominicbradbury.net/interviews.html

clxxix 'The Elveden Estate + Maharajah Duleep Singh', Lavender's Blue, posted 19 October 2104 - https://lvbmag.wordpress.com/2014/10/19/the-elveden-estate-maharajah-duleep-singh/

clxxx Ibid.

clxxxi Clive Aslet, 'Elveden Hall', Christie, Manson & Woods Ltd, 1984, p. 21.

clxxxii Ibid., p. 13.

clxxxiii 'One Man and his Empire', *Daily Telegraph*, 19 May 1985.

clxxxiv Clive Aslet, 'Elveden Hall', p. 15.

clxxxv Clive Aslet, 'Elveden Hall', , p. 21.

clxxxvi Pevsner, *The Buildings of England: Suffolk*, p. 200.

clxxxvii Byron Rogers, *Sunday Express*, 8 April 1984.

clxxxviii Axel, *The Nation's Tortured Body*, p. 69.

clxxxix Conversation with the author, March 2017.

cxc 'Vicar mediates over Punjabi maharajah statue argy-bhaji', *The Guardian*, 20 January 1993.

cxci 'In Pursuit of the Suffolk maharajah', *The Guardian*, 3 March 1993.

cxcii Ibid.

cxciii Ibid.

cxciv Ibid.

cxcv Tony Ballantyne, *Between Colonialism and Diaspora: Sikh Cultural Formations in an Imperial World* (Durham, North Carolina: Duke University Press, 2006), p. 110.

cxcvi Ibid., p. 110.

cxcvii Ibid., p. 114.

cxcviii See Howard Newby, *The Deferential Worker* (London: Viking, 1977).

Eight: To Thetford

cxcix Conversation with the author 23 January 2016.

cc 'Sikh-ing spot of Indian magic', *Eastern Daily Press*, 14 December 1992.

cci Ibid.

ccii 'In Pursuit of the Suffolk maharajah', *The Guardian*, 3 March 1993.

cciii Ibid.

cciv 'A Vital Night for Sikhs', *Thetford and Brandon Times*, 8 January 1993.

ccv Conversation with the author, 23 January 2016.

ccvi 'Memorial square to honour Sikh', *East Anglian Daily Times*, 13 May 1993.

ccvii 'Plan for equestrian statue of Sikh prince', *Thetford Times*, 2 July 1993.

ccviii 'Memorial square to honour Sikh', *East Anglian Daily Times*, 13 May 1993.

Nine: Butten Island

ccix For this account of Thetford's history I have relied almost entirely on Alan Crosby's excellent *A History of Thetford* (Chichester: Phillimore & Co. Ltd, 1986).

ccx Nikolaus Pevsner and Bill Wilson, *Norfolk 2: North-West and South* (London: Penguin Books, 1999), p 705.

ccxi Crosby, *A History of Thetford*, pp. 116-124.

ccxii Ibid., p. 122.

Ten: Centenary Celebrations

ccxiii 'Sikhs to attend special event', *Thetford Times*, 30 July 1993.

ccxiv 'Sikhs make Norfolk pilgrimage', *Eastern Daily Press*, 31 July 1993.

ccxv Conversation with author, 9 May 2017.

ccxvi 'Sikhs pay centenary tribute to last Maharaja,' *The Thetford Times*, 6 August 1993.

ccxvii 'Sikhs make Norfolk pilgrimage', *Eastern Daily Press*, 31 July 1993.

ccxviii 'Sikhs pay centenary tribute to last Maharaja,' *The Thetford Times*, 6 August 1993 and 'In Memory of the Black Prince', *Bury Free Press*, 6 August 1993.

ccxix 'Maharajah hailed a symbol of unity', *Thetford Times*, 29 October 1993.

Eleven: A Horse for the Maharajah

ccxx 'Prince's statue scheme backed', *Thetford and Watton Times*, 29 May 1997.

ccxxi 'Lasting memorial to honour Elveden's Black Prince', *Bury Free Press*, 2 August 1997.

ccxxii Conversation with the author, 28 November 2015.

ccxxiii Ibid.

ccxxiv Ibid.

ccxxv See her web site http://www.denisedutton.co.uk; the Duleep Singh statue is featured on the opening page.

ccxxvi 'Model of memorial to maharajah is unveiled', *Thetford and Watton Times*, 4 February 1998.

ccxxvii 'Sikhs pay homage to an exiled prince', *Bury Free Press*, 4 September 1998.

ccxxviii 'In Honour of A Prince', *Bury Free Press*, 28 August 1998.

ccxxix 'Statue gift from Sikhs', reference needed.

ccxxx Bance, *Sovereign, Squire & Rebel*, pp. 31 and p. 176.

Twelve: Contemplative Space

ccxxxi Note in Ancient House Museum archive.

ccxxxii Note in Ancient House Museum archive.

ccxxxiii https://en.wikipedia.org/wiki/Three-way_bridge

ccxxxiv It was lowered into position in September 1968 (*Thetford & Watton Times*, 27 September 1968, p8). The bridge was constructed by Boulton & Paul and won a structural steelwork award (*Thetford & Watton Times*, 10 October 1969, p1).

ccxxxv https://www.sikhs.org/khanda.htm

Thirteen: Prince to Prince

ccxxxvi 'Charles in ceremony to honour Prince of the Punjab', *East Anglian Daily Times*, 30 July 1999.

ccxxxvii Ibid.

ccxxxviii Ibid.

ccxxxix 'Statue honours Britain's first Sikh settler', *The Guardian*, 30 July 1999.

ccxl Prince Philip made one of his celebrated gaffes in the park by querying the number of dead recorded on the memorial marker. See http://www.independent.co.uk/news/sikhs-help-queen-save-face-in-amritsar-1235971.html. See also http://www.independent.co.uk/news/world/ghost-of-raj-massacre-haunts-the-queens-visit-to-amritsar-1246093.html

ccxli http://edition.cnn.com/2006/WORLD/europe/03/28/britain.camilla/

ccxlii Singh and Tatla, *Sikhs in Britain*, p. 212.

ccxliii https://www.princeofwales.gov.uk/media/speeches/speech-hrh-the-prince-of-wales-reception-mark-the-sikh-festival-of-vaisakhi-st-jamess

ccxliv See 'The Anglo Sikh Festival' – 'A Special Relationship' from Ancient House file.

ccxlv A. Martin Wainwright, 'Queen Victoria and the Maharaja Duleep Singh: Conflicting Identities in an Imperial Context', p. 70 - http://www.ohioacademyofhistory.org/wp-content/uploads/2013/04/Wainwright.pdf

ccxlvi Ibid., p.74.

ccxlvii Ibid., p. 77.

Fourteen: Maharajah Restored

ccxlviii Unfortunately, there is no system in place to count the Sikh visitors to the statue, museum and grave, but anecdotal evidence suggests that the Sikhs are consistently faithful to their last king and make the journey to Thetford and Elveden in substantial numbers.

ccxlix https://scroll.in/article/852791/in-delhi-statues-of-british-monarchs-have-been-trashed-left-to-rot-a-fitting-end-to-a-cruel-rule

ccl 'Sick vandals desecrate statue', *East Anglian Daily Times*, 14 March 2005.

ccli http://www.sikhtimes.com/news_031205a.html

cclii http://news.bbc.co.uk/1/hi/england/norfolk/4342973.stm

ccliii There is also a Scottish Sikh Heritage Trail, which features nine locations, including the National Library of Scotland and the Argyll and Sutherland Highlanders Museum at Stirling Castle. In 2012 another location was added to the Scottish Trail, following the restoration of the gravestone marking the burial place of Duleep Singh and Bamba Singh's first baby, who died in August 1865 less than a day old.

ccliv www.singhtwins.co.uk

cclv The Singh Twins, 'Casualty of War: Portrait of Maharajah Duleep Singh', Artists' Commentary.

cclvi Ibid.

cclvii 'The Singh Twins: how we freed the last Maharaja from the shackles of empire', *The Guardian*, 26 November 2014.

cclviii The Singh Twins, Artists' Commentary.

cclix Ibid.

cclx 'The Singh Twins: how we freed the last Maharaja from the shackles of empire', *The Guardian*, 26 November 2014.

cclxi Ibid.

cclxii Ibid.

cclxiii Conversation with the author, 5 December 2017.

cclxiv Singh and Tatla, *Sikhs in Britain*, p. 45.

cclxv Conversation with the author, 21 February 2017.

cclxvi Singh and Tatla, *Sikhs in Britain*, p. 214.

cclxvii Thomas Paine, 'Reflections on the Life and Death of Lord Clive', *Pennsylvania Magazine*, March, 1775.

cclxviii Thomas Paine, 'A Serious Thought', *Pennsylvania Magazine*, 18 October 1775.

cclxix Ibid.

INDEX

INDEX

INDEX